Enchantment of America
LAKES, HILLS
AND PRAIRIES
The Middlewestern States

(One in a series of eight books)

In this heartland of America, sparkling lakes and cool forests meet the rolling prairies.

More than once beneath a shallow sea, the land emerged and was home to huge frogs and giant salamanders and then to dinosaurs.

But a mile-thick sheet of ice moved across what is Canada, and fingers of ice reached almost to the Ohio River. Four times these glaciers advanced, and left a changed landscape, leveled and dotted with lakes.

Relics tell of early hunters who may have followed the mastodons and mammoths as they retreated before the ice.

Over a period of about 2,500 years, Mound Builders farmed the land. French explorers came through the Great Lakes and found Woodland Indians.

Fur traders and missionaries came. Settlers from many parts of the world brought skills and arts with them.

Life in these states now is marked by farming, dairying, manufacturing and transportation.

Many areas of historic significance and State Parks preserve the colorful past.

State maps and specific information on each state are included.

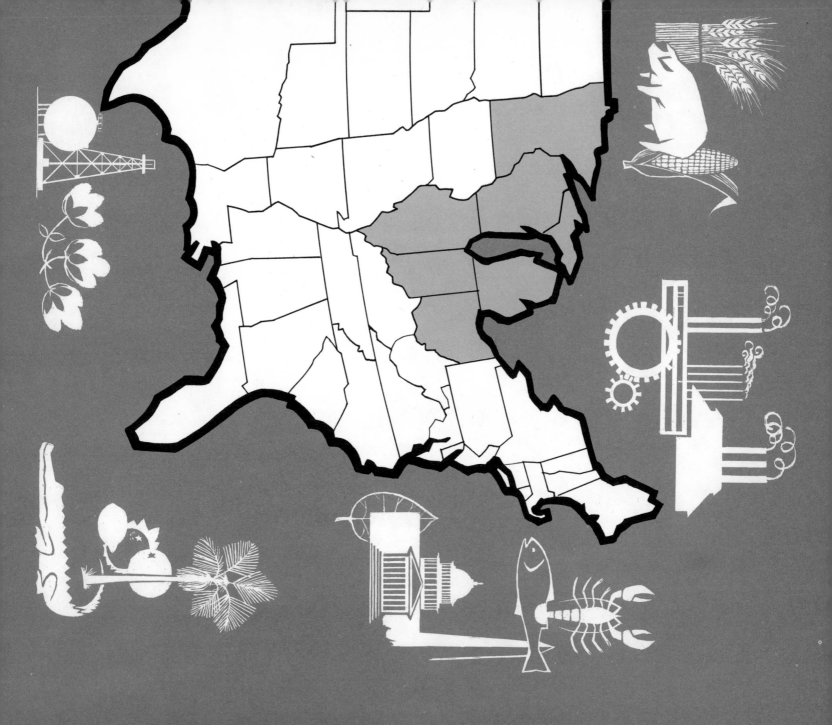

Enchantment of America

Lakes, Hills and Prairies

THE MIDDLEWESTERN STATES

Illinois • Indiana • Michigan • Minnesota • Ohio • Wisconsin

By Frances E. Wood

Illustrated by Tom Dunnington

CHILDRENS PRESS • CHICAGO

Educational Consultant for the
Enchantment of America Series:

Marilyn M. Spore, Laboratory School,

University of Chicago

Regional Consultant for

LAKES, HILLS AND PRAIRIES:

John D. Barnhart, Ph.D.,

Professor of History,

Indiana University

Contents

Location

In the six states of the Midwest that border the Great Lakes, sparkling lakes and waterfalls and cool green forests meet the placid prairies and fields of waving corn — truly an enchanted land. Ohio, Indiana, Michigan, Illinois, Wisconsin, and Minnesota are the Middlewestern States — the heartland of America.

Formation and Change

The rich prairie lands were formed over so long a period of time that it defies our imagination. Hundreds of millions of years ago, the interior lowlands of America were covered by shallow inland seas. Then, slowly, the land began to rise, inch by inch, and the sea retreated, only to creep in again when the land sank. This happened many times, and each time that the sea came in, it spread new layers of mud and sand and the lime of crushed sea shells. Rain washed more sediment into the sea. All of this was the beginning of the limestone and sandstone that underlie much of the Great Lakes region. Today the fossils of ancient sea animals and plants are often found in these sedimentary rocks.

Fish and other sea animals had been the only animals in the world, but now amphibians were starting to develop. These were animals that could live both in water and on the land. Creatures resembling huge frogs and giant salamanders became common. Enormous dragonflies flew about in the air, and other large insects appeared. The climate was warm and moist. The sea withdrew and left marshes and bogs where forests of giant, tree-like ferns and other strange tropical plants flourished.

Then the sea advanced again, burying the forests under mud and sand. Again and again this happened. Forests grew and were buried under water and heavy layers of sediment, which compressed the decaying plants into layers of hard black rock, or coal, as we know it today. Beds of coal underlie parts of Illinois, Indiana, Ohio, and Michigan. Fossils of ferns and other plants in the various rock layers help us to trace this amazing story.

As the centuries wore on, many kinds of egg-laying reptiles appeared, then small dinosaurs, and finally huge ones that were supreme on land and in the water. These gave way, at last, to the warm-blooded mammals, most of which were covered with hair and bore their young alive instead of hatching them from eggs. Some of these mammals were the forerunners of many of our animals today.

By the time that warm-blooded animals became common, about sixty million years ago, the sea had withdrawn for the last time from the interior of North America. The climate became cooler, and the marshes dried up. Mountain building was going on in the west, while, in the east, the forces of erosion were wearing down the ancient Appalachians and carrying some of the material from them onto the interior lowlands.

The Ice Age

About one million years ago, conditions arose which changed the whole course of events for the area we now know as the Great Lakes region. The climate became colder and colder, and the summers became shorter and shorter. So much snow fell in the north that it could not melt. A great ice sheet was formed, a mile or more thick, which began moving slowly south across what is now Canada and the northern United States. Long fingers of ice reached nearly as far south as the Ohio River and southern Illinois. As the ice sheet moved, it picked up rocks and dirt and other debris and carried them along. It scraped off the tops of hills and deposited them in valleys, and it spread a thick layer of soil over the prairies. This material left by moving ice, or glaciers, is called "drift."

The trees of that time were much like those we know today, such as spruce, oak, maple, walnut, locust, and alder. As the glaciers moved

southward across the forests, they snapped the trees off as if they were matches and buried them under tons of ice and debris.

Four times the glaciers advanced, and four times they retreated again into the North. In the intervals between the advance and retreat of the ice, the climate became mild again and forests grew up and flourished, only to be covered by the ice once more.

During the Ice Age, numerous mammals ranged over most of North America — horses, camels, deer, wolves, saber-toothed tiger cats, beavers as large as black bears, giant ground sloths, and many other animals. Giant bison, deer, bears, and mammoths entered this continent from Asia by way of a narrow bridge of land, or, perhaps, an ice-bridge between Siberia and Alaska.

As the glaciers advanced, the animals retreated southward. Only a few of the more hardy ones — some of the mastodons and woolly mammoths, the musk ox and reindeer — stayed near the ice. All the other animals were crowded into the southern areas. Each time the ice melted, they moved north again, to be driven back when the glaciers advanced.

This went on for thousands and thousands of years. Before it ended — and some people think it has not ended yet — many kinds of animals had disappeared. The saber-toothed tigers and the giant beavers were gone forever. Horses, which had migrated to most parts of the world, became extinct on this continent and did not reappear until they were brought to America by the Spaniards thousands of years later. The mastodons and mammoths, which were the forerunners of elephants, may have existed for a short time after the Ice Age. But soon they, too, disappeared, perhaps wiped out by human hunters, who had appeared in America during the latter part of the Ice Age.

The ice advanced for the last time about 25,000 years ago, and it melted from the Great Lakes area less than 10,000 years ago. When it melted, it left a changed landscape. Except for great piles of rock and dirt, called "moraines," which the glaciers had dropped here and there, the land was level. Dotting the area were thousands of lakes, formed by melting ice in hollows scooped out by the glaciers or in river valleys blocked by moraines.

The Great Lakes

The Great Lakes are by far the largest of the numerous glacial lakes that remain today — in fact, they are the largest fresh-water lakes in the world. Of the five lakes — Superior, Michigan, Huron, Erie, and Ontario — Lake Michigan is the only one that lies entirely within the United States. All the others are shared with Canada. Lake Superior is much the largest and deepest of the lakes and has the highest water level — over 600 feet above sea level. Ontario, the smallest lake, also has the lowest water level — only 247 feet.

Many small rivers flow into the lakes; until the beginning of this century, however, only the St. Lawrence River drained them. In 1900 the course of the Chicago River was reversed. Instead of flowing into Lake Michigan as it once did, it now flows out of the lake, through the Chicago Sanitary and Ship Canal, into the Illinois Waterway and the Mississippi River.

Taken together, these five lakes form the greatest inland waterway in the world, and so have been a tremendous influence on the life and history of our country. The Indians used them before the white man set foot on their shores. French explorers and fur traders penetrated deep into the interior of our country by means of them. Great cities and ports have sprung up along their shores, and their wide, shining beaches have furnished recreation and relaxation to millions of people.

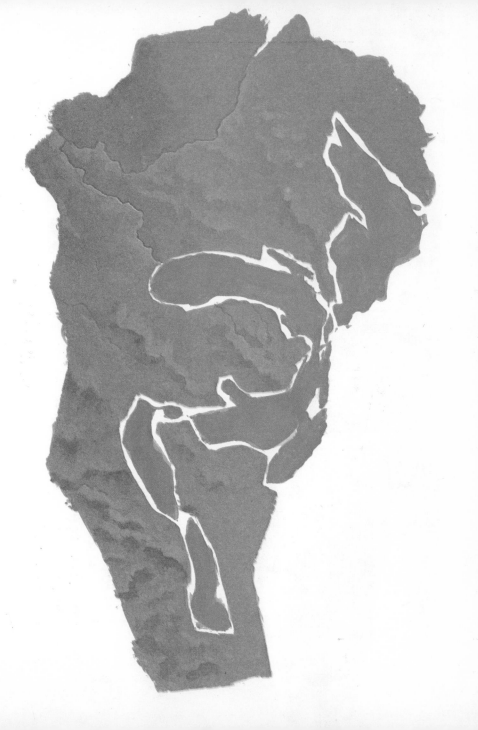

The Lay of the Land Today

The Canadian Shield, which covers more than half of Canada, extends southward into the northernmost states of the Lakes region. This low plateau, also called the Laurentian Plateau, is shaped somewhat like an enormous shield. It is composed largely of very ancient rocks and was heavily scoured by glaciers during the Ice Age. Much of the soil was scraped off and spread over the prairie regions. Thick forests cover much of the plateau in Minnesota, Wisconsin, and Michigan, and thousands of glacial lakes make the region a "water wonderland." In Minnesota and Michigan the "roots" of very old mountains, worn down by erosion, contain iron, copper, and other valuable metals.

The Allegheny Plateau, a part of the Appalachian Highlands, covers the east half of Ohio, and a spur of the Ozark Mountains juts across the southern tip of Illinois.

Except for these few highlands, this mid-west region is largely made up of gently rolling plains, forming some of the richest farming land in America. Here and there the flatness of the landscape is broken by low hills or rocky glacial moraines. A famous one, the Valparaiso Moraine, extends in a series of hills, ridges, and valleys around Lake Michigan from the Chicago area into Indiana and Michigan. This moraine at one time impounded melting waters of the ice sheet, to form a much larger lake than Lake Michigan is today. Water once covered the flat area where Chicago now stands. Scientists call this prehistoric body of water "Lake Chicago." Shifting sand dunes border the wide beaches of the present Lake Michigan.

14

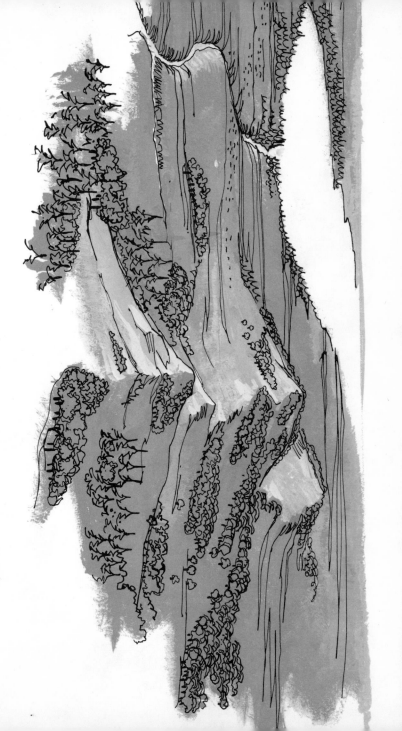

A section in southwestern Wisconsin and the extreme northwestern corner of Illinois, called the "Driftless Area," was never covered by the glaciers. In this section, which was protected by highlands to the north, are buttes and pinnacles of rock, high hills and deep valleys. There are few lakes. This small, picturesque, unglaciated area is in marked contrast to the glaciated country surrounding it, where the leveling work of the ice sheets is plain to be seen.

In northwestern Minnesota, a flat section with fertile soil is part of the dry floor of an enormous prehistoric lake, formed toward the end of the Ice Age, when ice temporarily blocked the Red River of the North, which separates Minnesota and North Dakota. Lake Winnipeg in Canada, Lake of the Woods, and many smaller lakes are remnants of this ancient lake, called Lake Agassiz.

The river systems of the Middlewestern States drain in three different directions. Some reach the Atlantic by way of the Great Lakes and the St. Lawrence River; others join the Mississippi on its way south to the Gulf of Mexico. The Red River of the North, with its tributaries, flows north, through Lake Winnipeg, to Hudson Bay.

15

The Mighty Mississippi

The Mississippi forms the western boundary of Illinois and part of Wisconsin. With its tributaries, it is one of the greatest river systems in the world and with the Missouri forms the longest river in the United States. The source of this mighty river is at Lake Itasca, in north-central Minnesota. Here, where it leaves the lake, it is so small that you can wade across it. At first it flows north and then east, through several lakes, before it turns south and begins its long journey to the Gulf of Mexico. It grows larger and larger, as other streams empty into it. At St. Paul, where the Minnesota River joins it, the Mississippi becomes navigable. For much of its course in Wisconsin and Illinois, the river is marked by steep limestone bluffs and palisades.

Near St. Louis, Missouri, just across the river from Illinois, the Missouri joins the Mississippi, and at the southern tip of Illinois another famous river, the Ohio, becomes part of the Mississippi. Because they were navigable, both rivers were important in the exploration and settlement of mid-America.

During periodic spring floods, the Mississippi and Ohio and their tributaries, have wrought great damage to the towns and farms in their valleys. Although dams and levees have been built to prevent floods, the rivers continue to overflow their banks during periods of high water.

Climate

Because of their location in the interior of the continent, separated from the oceans by mountains, the Middlewestern States have what we call a "continental" climate; that is, they have long, cold winters and short, hot summers. The northern states have colder winters, with more snow, than the more southern states; as a rule, the summers are also cooler, especially at night. As far south as northern Illinois and Indiana, however, winter winds often pile up the snow into great drifts, stopping traffic until the drifts are cleared away by snowplows.

The areas that border the Great Lakes are usually not quite so cold in the winter nor so warm in the summer as those away from the lakes. That is because it takes water longer to absorb heat than it does land, and water also loses its heat more slowly. So, in the summer, cool lake breezes often bring relief to the hot land, while in the winter, warmer air from the lakes moderates frigid weather.

Sometimes a winter wind, blowing across Lake Michigan from the northwest, is warmed and picks up an unusual amount of moisture. When this moisture-laden wind reaches the colder land, it dumps so much snow on the lake's east shore that it sometimes takes the residents several days to dig out.

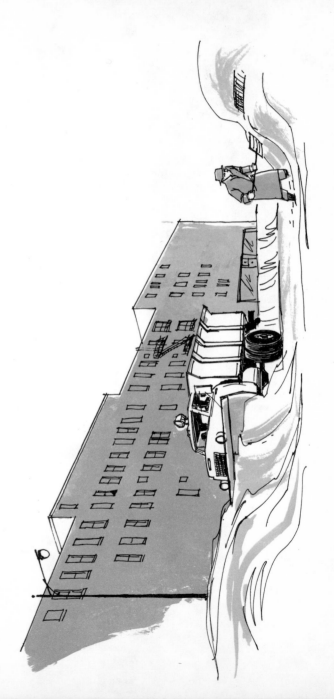

Autumn in the Middlewestern States is beautiful; many of the days are warm and sunny, and the nights cool and comfortable. This is the season when the hardwood forests are a blaze of color and the geese are honking overhead on their way south.

Rainfall ranges from 29 inches in the drier west to 40 inches and more in the humid eastern and southern sections. The growing season is as short as 80 days in the extreme north and reaches 180 to 200 days in the warmer areas.

Things to think about

In what different ways were the prairies, lakes and hills formed?

How was the face of the land different at the end of the Ice Age?

How do the Great Lakes affect the climate of the Lakes region?

People come to the land of lakes

The First People

Sometime during the latter part of the Ice Age, at least 25,000 years ago, man entered the New World from Siberia over a land or ice bridge across Bering Strait into Alaska. This passage which separates Alaska from the eastern tip of Siberia, is little more than 50 miles wide and less than 150 feet deep. During the Ice Age, sea level was 200 to 300 feet lower than it is now, and at times the floor of Bering Strait was a land bridge that connected the two continents.

The first people who crossed the bridge of land or ice were probably small groups of hunters who followed giant bison and mammoths to the new continent. The Yukon Valley in Alaska was not covered by ice, and the newcomers found rich hunting indeed — not only the huge beasts they had been following, but camels and horses and other animals native to the New World.

The bones of many animals around the charred remains of camp-fires and the stone weapons and other relics of these ancient hunters tell their fascinating story. As is the way with hunters, they were con-stantly on the move and followed their game along river valleys and through mountain passes. Then they gradually moved south along the eastern foot of the Rocky Mountains, where there was a wide area free from ice, and spread eastward as the interior ice sheet melted. Traces of these early migrants have been found as far east as the Atlantic Coast, and southward through Mexico and Central America to the tip of South America.

During part of this time the area around the Great Lakes was covered by ice, which advanced and retreated several times. The hunters followed the herds of mammoths and mastodons which wandered along the melting edges of the glaciers, moving south when the ice advanced and north as it melted again. The skeleton of a fifteen-year-old girl, found buried deep in the dry bed of an ancient Minnesota lake, may have lain there for 20,000 years.

There is little information available concerning man in the New World for a period of several thousand years following the end of the Ice Age. Most of the big-game animals disappeared during the last of the Ice Age or shortly thereafter, and the day of the mighty hunter was over. Families learned to exist on berries and nuts, the seeds and roots of edible plants, and such small game as they could kill. They often lived in caves.

In various parts of North and South America, people began to cultivate certain kinds of wild plants and to grow better ones. Somewhere, perhaps in Mexico or Central America, maize, which we call corn, was developed from a wild plant. Indians brought some of the seed north to the Mississippi Valley and elsewhere. Wild squash and pumpkins were also cultivated, and, later, beans. And so farming came to the region of the Great Lakes.

The Mound Builders

About a thousand years before the birth of Christ, a new Indian culture appeared in the Mississippi Valley and eventually spread all over the eastern half of what is now the United States. This was the culture of the people we call the "Mound Builders." They built the thousands and thousands of earth mounds that are found in the Middle-western States and all up and down the Mississippi and Ohio valleys.

Although we apply the same name to all of these people, the Mound Builders actually represent the many different kinds of Indians who built various types of earthworks over a period of at least 2,500 years.

The burial mounds are the most common ones found in the Middle-western States today. These range all the way from small round and cone-shaped ones, 20 to 30 feet high, to elaborate groupings, covering 100 or more acres. Some of the mounds in the groups are circular and semi-circular; others are square or octagon-shaped. Still more elaborate earthworks, probably used for ceremonial purposes, are shaped like animals, such as turtles, snakes, bears, foxes, and various kinds of birds. A good example of these is the Serpent Mound in Ohio, which is approximately a quarter of a mile long.

Another kind of mound, called the "temple mound," appeared much later. The first ones were probably built about five hundred years after the birth of Christ, and southeastern Indians were still building these in the sixteenth century, when De Soto and other Spanish explorers entered the area. Only a few temple mounds are found as far north as the Lakes region, two famous ones being the Aztalán Mound near Madison, Wisconsin, and the Cahokia Group near East St. Louis, Illinois.

The temple mounds are square or oblong, with terraced sides and flat tops, where wooden structures once stood. The wood has rotted away and disappeared long since. Although made of earth, these mounds are similar in size and shape to the great stone pyramids found in Mexico and Central America. These pyramids were the bases for the magnificent temples and palaces of the Aztec and Mayan Indians.

Some of the mounds are so large that it must have taken thousands of workmen many years to build them. The bull dozers and other heavy machinery that we use today to move large quantities of earth were unknown in the days of the Mound Builders. In fact, even the wheel was unknown, and there were no horses or other domestic animals in the New World at this time. All of the dirt in these huge earthworks had to be carried in baskets, some of it for long distances.

The burial mounds were used for important leaders and priests. Beautifully ornamented robes, woven from plant fibers, were wrapped around the bodies, which were then placed in log tombs in the burial mound. Handsome copper breastplates and headdresses, stone tools and weapons, beautifully carved stone pipes, and many other treasures were put around the bodies. Then earth was piled on the tombs. Sometimes the tomb was burned and the body cremated before the earth was piled on.

The many beautiful objects found in and around the mounds show that the Mound Builders had great skill and artistic ability. These objects, which we call "artifacts," also show that each tribe of Indians traded with other tribes all over the country. Burial mounds in Ohio, for example, contained artifacts that had been brought from every direction.

Necklaces were made of sea shells and the teeth of sharks and alligators that came from the Atlantic Seacoast and the Gulf of Mexico. Obsidian, a very hard black volcanic glass which was much prized

for making knives and spear points and arrowheads, was brought from the Yellowstone area in the West. Copper, used to make breastplates, headdresses, bracelets, and other ornaments, came from Isle Royale, in Lake Superior. The old copper mines which were worked by the Indians and the crude "hammerstones" which they used to separate the copper from the rock, are preserved in Isle Royale National Park.

The Mound Builders lived in small villages near their mounds and raised beans, squash and pumpkins, corn, and tobacco. Fishing was especially good in the Great Lakes area, and deer, bear, and other game were plentiful so food was easy to obtain. Village sites are still marked by the remains of cooking fires and trash heaps containing ashes, bones of animals, broken tools and pottery, and other household items.

Later mounds and the artifacts found in them show that, as the centuries went by, the Mound Builders lost some of their skill and artistic ability, and their culture declined. We do not know exactly why this happened, nor what became of these people. Perhaps more primitive tribes moved into their area and gradually absorbed them. Be that as it may, the Indians who were here when the first European explorers arrived in the Great Lakes region were much more primitive than the Mound Builders and did not remember them at all.

French Explorers, Traders and Missionaries

The first white men to see the Great Lakes were French explorers, who had entered the New World through the St. Lawrence River and established a small settlement at Quebec in Canada. They penetrated the lake country by means of the waterways, as the Indians had done for centuries.

Fur traders and missionaries followed on the heels of the explorers and made friends with the Indians whom they found there. Missions were set up in the wilderness. Military forts and trading posts were established which became the center for small settlements. The fur traders traveled along the rivers and shores of the lakes in canoes and bartered knives, blankets, mirrors, beads, and ribbons to the Indians for valuable furs.

26

Woodland Indians

These Indians were different from the Mound Builders, who had long since disappeared. Most of the area was covered by dense forests, and we call the people who inhabited them "Woodland Indians." They gathered wild rice, berries, nuts, and herbs, and made sugar from maple sap; they practiced agriculture, raising corn and squash and beans. They also fished and hunted wild game, and trapped fur-bearing animals.

Their dome-shaped wigwams were made of poles covered with bark mats, and their birch canoes were so light that they could easily be carried around rapids or from one stream to another.

The Woodland Indians around the Great Lakes belonged to a great Indian family called the Algonquians, some of whom may have descended from the Mound Builders. The Algonquian family was made up of many different tribes, such as the Chippewa or Ojibwa, the Pota-

watomi, the Miami, the Menominee, the Sauk and Fox, the Shawnee, and the Delaware.

Toward the east, fierce Indian tribes belonging to the Iroquois family invaded the Ohio Valley and settled in northern Ohio and southern Michigan, in the Detroit area. Siouan tribes, called Dakotas, lived in the upper Mississippi Valley until they were driven out by the Chippewas and encroaching white settlers and forced to join their kinsmen on the Great Plains.

Father Jacques Marquette, a Jesuit missionary who had established missions at Sault Ste. Marie and near the Straits of Mackinac, heard much from the Indians about the wide river that flowed south, clear to the sea. Finally, in 1673, he and a young fur trader named Louis Jolliet determined to find this great river.

Down the Mississippi

With five French *voyageurs*, or boatmen, Marquette and Jolliet crossed Green Bay and traveled down the Fox River. From there they carried their canoes along an Indian trail to the Wisconsin River and floated down it until at last they reached the Mississippi — the wide and beautiful river they had heard so much about! Continuing down the Mississippi, they passed the mouths of the Missouri and Ohio rivers, and came to the mouth of the Arkansas. Here they turned back because they were afraid of unfriendly Indians and the Spaniards who had laid claim to the Gulf Coast.

Marquette and Jolliet returned by way of the Illinois and Des Plaines rivers, making friends with the Indians along their route. They portaged to Lake Michigan across the area where Chicago now stands.

Some years later, Robert Cavelier, Sieur de La Salle, another famous French explorer and fur trader, explored the Mississippi River to its mouth and claimed for France all the land drained by the river. He named this vast area Louisiana in honor of the French king. His hope was to found a great French empire in the heart of the North American continent. Forts and missions were built in the Great Lakes area and along the Illinois and Mississippi rivers, but the settlements around them never became very large, because only a relatively small number of French came to America. About this time, also, the first of a series of four wars with England occupied the attention of France.

In 1701, following the end of the first war with England, a French explorer named Antoine Cadillac founded a fortified settlement on the spot where Detroit now stands.

30

Wars Between France and England

The French claimed the area between the Ohio River and the Great Lakes, but were slow to move into it, partly because of the unfriendly attitude of the Iroquois Indians who hunted and fought in the region.

The English also claimed the area, and England gave the Ohio Land Company a large land grant in the rich Ohio Valley.

When the French began building a string of forts along the Ohio River, an expedition of British soldiers and Virginia colonials, led by General Edward Braddock, was sent against them. Aided by Algonquian Indians, the French nearly wiped out the expedition, and Braddock was killed. George Washington, one of the colonial officers, was among the few who escaped.

The fourth and last war between France and England soon followed. This was bitterly fought in America and was known as the French and Indian War, because the Indians took an important part in it. The Algonquians fought on the side of the French, and the Iroquois with the English, and a fierce struggle ensued. In the end, the English were victorious, and the French lost all their land in the New World east of the Mississippi except the small Ile d' Orléans in the St. Lawrence River.

The victors were in immediate trouble with the Algonquians, however, who much preferred the French to the English. Pontiac, a famous Ottawa chief, attempted to unite all the Indian tribes and kill every white person west of the Alleghenies. He succeeded in destroying a number of English forts, but gave up when he failed to take the important fort at Detroit. The Indians continued to harass and kill the settlers, however, whenever they could.

Settlers for the Northwest Territory

Following the American Revolution, England ceded all of her land east of the Mississippi and south of Canada to the new nation. The northwestern section of this land, which England had taken away from France, became known as the Northwest Territory. It included all of the land of the Middlewestern States except that part of Minnesota west of the Mississippi, which was obtained from France when President Jefferson purchased the Louisiana Territory in 1803.

Prior to the Revolution, England had discouraged settlement of the West, partly because of Indians, but also because she wanted the rich fur trade to continue, and wide-spread settlement would result in the elimination of most of the fur-bearing animals. As soon as the new nation was established, however, and the Northwest Territory opened for settlement, people began pouring into the Ohio Valley. Marietta, the first permanent white settlement in Ohio, was founded in 1788 at the junction of the Muskingum and Ohio rivers, and Losantiville, later renamed Cincinnati, rose a few months later.

Some of the settlers arrived in covered wagons, but many came down the Ohio River in flatboats. These boats were square, boxlike structures, with flat bottoms, and usually contained living quarters for the settlers and sheds for their stock, as well as plenty of cargo space. The settlers would float down the river in the boats, and then, when they reached their new lands, would often use the lumber in the boats for building their houses.

The Indians did not take kindly to the coming of so many white men. Instead of buying their furs and giving them guns and whisky and trinkets as the fur traders had done, the newcomers settled on their lands and drove the wild game from their forests. Unprovoked acts of cruelty toward the Indians added fuel to the flames, and many settlers were killed or frightened away.

Not until General "Mad Anthony" Wayne had defeated the Indians in the Battle of Fallen Timbers in 1794 and made the Greenville Treaty with them the following year, were the settlers safe from attack. Then they came by the thousands, many of them pressing on into Indiana and Illinois. In 1803, Fort Dearborn was founded on the present site of Chicago.

"Johnny Appleseed"

In the river valleys of Ohio and, later, in Indiana, the newcomers often found that a man had preceded them and started nurseries of young apple trees in the wilderness. From these nurseries, the settlers could start apple orchards of their own. Since apples were an important item in the diet of the pioneers, this man became an important and well-loved personage. He was welcome at every fireside, where he told enthralling stories of the wilderness. He made friends with the Indians, too, and moved among them without ever being harmed. His name was John Chapman, but many knew him only by his nickname, "Johnny Appleseed," and many legends were woven about him, so that he has become a major figure in the folklore of the region.

34

Another War

Although England had ceded the land to the United States at the end of the Revolution, British fur traders were slow to give up the area that is now Michigan and Wisconsin. British troops continued to occupy the forts and incite the Indians against the American traders and settlers. Following Wayne's victory at Fallen Timbers, the British soldiers withdrew from Detroit and other forts, but reoccupied them for a time during the War of 1812.

In this war, the Indians again sided with the British and carried on bitter warfare against the Americans, hoping to drive them from the Northwest. Indians in Illinois massacred the garrison at Fort Dearborn and burned the fort, and those in the Ohio Valley once more waged a campaign of terror against the settlers. When America won the war, the Indians left Ohio forever, some withdrawing to Canada and others moving farther west. In other areas they were gradually pushed west of the Mississippi River or moved onto reservations.

New Roads and Waterways

In the first ten years after the War of 1812, the population doubled in the Ohio Valley and around the Great Lakes. At that time this region was called "the West." The farmers raised a great surplus of farm products in the rich soil, and needed some way to reach the eastern and southern markets.

In the early 1800's there were no roads through the wilderness. Pioneers followed the narrow Indian trails and the wider paths, or "traces," made by the buffalo. The Cumberland, or National, Road was the first, and for a long time the only road built by the national government. It started at Cumberland, Maryland, and by 1818 had reached Wheeling, West Virginia, thus joining the Potomac and Ohio rivers. It was later turned over to the states and extended through Ohio and Indiana to Vandalia, Illinois, where it ended.

Another important development in transportation was the completion in 1825 of the Erie Canal, which the state of New York built between the Hudson River and Lake Erie, a distance of about 365 miles. This provided water transportation all the way from the Great Lakes to the Atlantic Seaboard.

The first boats were towed by horses and mules that walked along a path beside the canal. The average speed for these horse- and mule-drawn boats was about one-and-a-half miles per hour. The Erie Canal brought much trade to the area around the Great Lakes, and the towns that sprang up along it grew rapidly. The canal was widened and deepened several times, and is today part of the New York State Barge Canal.

The common mode of travel on the rivers was by flatboat, which floated easily down the streams but would not go up them. When a farmer floated his produce down to market, he usually sold the flatboat for the lumber in it and then walked home over Indian trails.

The keelboat was a long, narrow boat with sharp ends. It could return upstream, but it took a crew of strong men armed with stout poles to push it against the current.

Since Fulton's steamboat, the *Clermont*, had made its trial run on the Hudson River in 1807, men had been working to make the steam-boat practical for western rivers. With the coming of the *New Orleans* to the Ohio and the Mississippi in 1811, a new era started in the Mid-west, for steamboats like this one could travel up the rivers as well as

down them. And they could travel on the Great Lakes, too. As fast as new boats could be built, they were put to work carrying freight and passengers on the rivers and lakes.

Even so, some of the farmers continued to use flatboats. Abraham Lincoln, who had moved with his family from Indiana to Illinois in 1830, once helped to pilot a flatboat loaded with produce down the Illinois and Mississippi rivers to New Orleans.

With the Erie Canal and with steamboats on the rivers and the Great Lakes, soon followed by railroads, the states of the Lakes region became more and more prosperous. Chicago, which had started as a small settlement around Fort Dearborn, at the foot of Lake Michigan, mushroomed into a great city. By the 1860's it was already the railroad capital of the nation, with railroads coming in from the east and the south and going out to the west.

Things to think about

How did it happen that the first people turned from hunting to farming?

Compare and explain the different types of mounds that were built in the Midwest.

Why did the first white men come to the Lakes region? How were the Indians living at this time?

What happened when the Northwest Territory was opened for settlement?

What made the Midwest a center of transportation even in the 1800's? What were some of the early means of transportation in this region?

Life in the lake states today

Natural Resources

The deep, rich soil spread over the Middlewestern States by glaciers is only one of their many valuable natural resources. Iron ore, mined from the remnants of ancient, worn-down mountains in the north, and coal beds underlying Illinois, Michigan, Ohio, and Indiana, have made possible the great steel mills and other heavy industries of the Midwest. Copper, found in Michigan's Upper Peninsula, and limestone, sandstone, petroleum, gas, salt, and other minerals contribute to the prosperity of the region. The Great Lakes and navigable streams provide an economical means of getting agricultural and industrial products to market. And these great waterways, together with thousands of smaller lakes and streams, help bring an enormous tourist trade to the states of the Great Lakes region.

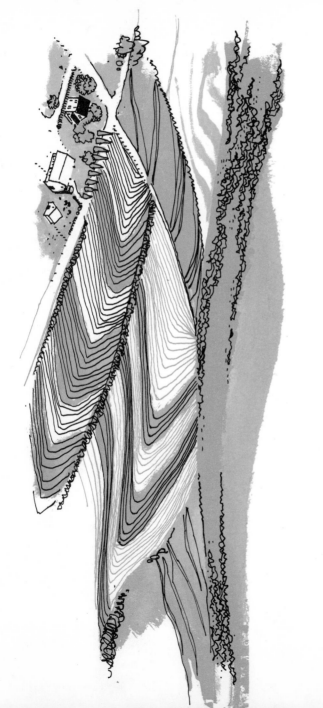

Farming and Dairying

When the first pioneers entered the region between the Allegheny Plateau and the Mississippi, they found a level area of deep forests and rich soil. Those who pushed on through Ohio and Indiana into Illinois rode through buffalo grass higher than their stirrups. They called Illinois "the Prairie State," although it, too, had many trees growing deep along the streams and scattered in small groves among the prairies.

At first the settlers built their homes and cleared their fields in the more familiar groves and river bottoms, as they had done in the areas they left behind, for they did not know how to cope with the tough buffalo grass. As more and more people arrived, however, some of them were forced to settle on the prairies, and they soon learned that the prairie soil was rich and easy to cultivate.

The pioneers found that the lake and prairie region, with its rich soil and humid climate, was ideal for growing crops. It quickly became the greatest food-producing area in the nation, and continues to hold that title. When we fly over the area today, instead of the dense forests and tall buffalo grass that once covered the land below us, we look down on a vast checkerboard of cultivated farms. On many of them we see dairy cattle and other livestock feeding.

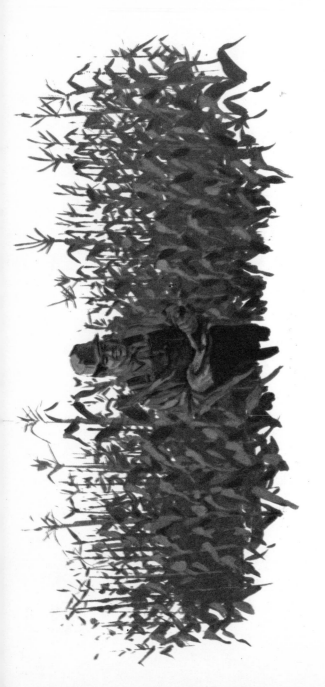

The white man had learned from the Indian how to grow and process many kinds of food, such as corn, peanuts, tobacco, maple sugar, beans, tomatoes, sweet corn, squash, pumpkins, potatoes, and sweet potatoes. The "western" pioneers grew all of these crops, and, as time went on, grew them better and better.

Today the Indians' small patches of corn and beans and squash have grown into far-flung fields of waving corn and huge truck farms and orchards that fill millions of cans with vegetables and fruit. The finest corn in the world is grown in the area we call the "Corn Belt," of which the Middlewestern States form a large part. These states are famous, too, for such important crops as hay, wheat, oats, and soybeans. Especially fine fruit — apples, peaches, cherries, blueberries, strawberries, and grapes — is grown near the lakes, where the climate is tempered by lake breezes.

Food is shipped from the Middlewestern States to points all over the world. Some of it is fed to livestock — cattle, sheep, hogs, and poultry. Some of the animals are raised right on the farms that produce the crops. Much of the livestock, however, especially cattle and sheep, is brought in from the western plains to be fattened up before being turned into steaks and chops and roasts for our dinner tables. Some of the fodder crops are fed to dairy cattle and help to produce the cream, butter, cheese, and other dairy products for which Wisconsin and Minnesota are famous.

40

Mining

Indians were the first miners in the Midwest, as well as the first farmers. For centuries they mined the red stone for their peace pipes from the famous Pipestone Quarry in southwestern Minnesota. Long famous in Chippewa and Sioux legends, the quarry is still reserved for the use of the Indians. It is now a part of the Pipestone National Monument.

Many ornaments and other articles made of copper were found among the artifacts of the Mound Builders. The first copper mined by white men in the Great Lakes area was on the Keweenaw Peninsula, with Copper Harbor as the center of operations. This Michigan peninsula, which juts into Lake Superior southeast of Isle Royale, contained some of the richest copper mines in the world, and at one time supplied half of all the copper mined in the United States. Although the heyday of copper mining in Michigan is over, the state still ships out some high-grade copper.

The enormous deposits of both high-grade and low-grade iron ore in the northern highlands of Michigan and Minnesota have brought world renown to these states. Some of the iron ore is deep within the earth, but much of it lies close to the surface. To reach it, the miners need only to strip off the glacial drift deposited there by the ice sheets that once covered the area. Some of the greatest open-pit or "strip" mines in the world are in Minnesota's Mesabi Range.

Coal is the leading mineral product in the southern section of the Midwest, in Illinois, Indiana, and Ohio, with some in Michigan; oil is also found in these four states. Clay is an important mineral, especially in Ohio, and salt is mined in Ohio and Michigan. Limestone is prevalent throughout the Lakes region, but most of the limestone that is used for building purposes throughout the United States is furnished by the oölitic limestone quarries of Indiana. "Oölitic" comes from the Greek word meaning "eggstone," and the limestone is so named because it is made up of small round grains that look like fish eggs.

Lumbering

The settlers who first came to the Lakes region did not realize what a rich heritage they had in the great forests that covered most of the area. Their only thought was to clear the land as quickly as possible and plant it in crops that would provide food for themselves and their livestock. They used some of the trees they cut down to build homes,

fences, and for the fuel for their fireplaces. The rest they destroyed to get them out of the way.

As more and more settlers arrived, more lumber was needed to build settlements and forts to protect them. Towns sprang up throughout the Ohio and Mississippi valleys, and the population spread farther and farther west. With the coming of steamboats and railroads, transportation of lumber to faraway markets became possible, and a vast lumbering industry swept across the Midwest, razing the forests as it went. Hundreds of sawmills, powered first by water wheels and then by steam, appeared along the rivers. Whole forests of logs floated down to the mills to be sawed into planks. Strong, lusty lumberjacks became the heroes of young America, and from them came the "tall" stories of the mighty Paul Bunyan and his blue ox, Babe.

Not until almost all the forests were gone, and the lumbermen had moved on, did the people of the Lakes region realize their loss. Now state and national governments cooperate in an effort to reforest some of the cutover areas. In national and state forests only certain marked trees are cut. As the new forests are thinned or land is cleared in order to plant better trees, great quantities of small trees are shipped to pulp mills to be made into paper.

Manufacturing and Industry

In the days of French occupancy and during the region's early years as the Northwest Territory, practically the only industry of the Great Lakes area was its rich fur trade. As the settlers and lumbermen came in and cut down the forests, the fur-bearing animals moved north, and lumbering became the big business of the day. Low-cost transportation and nearness to the source of raw materials brought a great era of manufacturing and heavy industry to the Midwest and helped make Chicago the second-largest city in the nation.

The steel mills that day and night belch forth their smoke and flames along the southern shores of Lake Michigan and Lake Erie are fed from the iron ore and limestone of Michigan and Minnesota. Much of the steel from the mills goes to the great automobile plants of Detroit, called the automobile capital of the world. It goes, too, to other important automobile plants in Mid-America and to manufacturers of airplane parts, farm and road machinery, tools, household appliances, and hundreds of other products that have made the Middle-western States famous for industry.

Furniture is an important product, and Grand Rapids, Michigan, has become known as the furniture capital of the nation. Battle Creek is the "breakfast food city." Minneapolis is noted for its huge flour mills, and its twin city, St. Paul, has large meat-packing plants. Wisconsin is famous for her butter and cheese, and her chief lake port, Milwaukee, is noted for its breweries. The huge printing and publishing industry of Chicago and other Midwest cities receives much of its paper from the paper mills of the northern Lakes area.

Ohio leads the nation in the making of pottery, as well as in the manufacture of tires and many other articles made from rubber. This state also specializes in such unique products as matches, playing cards, false teeth, cash registers, and Fiberglas. One well-known article made from Fiberglas is the glass boat, popular on Mid-America's many lakes and streams.

The needs of World Wars I and II speeded up manufacturing in the Midwest. While men went to war, many women took their places in the steel mills and factories so that there would be no slackening in the production of defense materials. The Middlewestern States also have a large share in the electronics industry that has developed since the wars, and in the manufacture of products vital to national security and to the "atoms-for-peace" program.

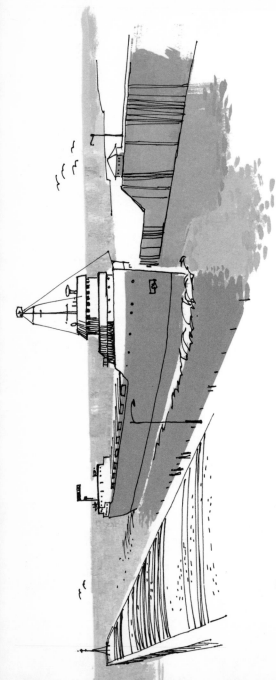

Transportation

The states of the Lakes region are the hub of the nation's great transportation system, which carries Mid-America's agricultural and industrial products to all parts of the world. Huge barges ply the Great Lakes and each year move more than twice as much freight through the Soo Locks between Lake Superior and Lake Huron than goes through the Panama Canal.

From the time they were used by explorers and fur traders to penetrate to the very heart of the great new land, the lakes and rivers of the area have been important in the development of the country. Sailing schooners preceded steamboats on the lakes. The completion of the Erie Canal brought people by the thousands from the eastern seaboard. Now the St. Lawrence Seaway brings ships from all over the world to inland ports.

In 1959, Queen Elizabeth came from England to help the President of the United States, Dwight Eisenhower, dedicate the Seaway, which was built by Canada and the United States. The completion of the Seaway enables large, ocean-going vessels to go up the St. Lawrence River and across the Great Lakes to Chicago and other ports. They go from one lake to another by means of rivers, straits, and canals that connect the lakes. Locks in Canada's Welland Canal take shipping around Niagara Falls, between Lake Ontario and Lake Erie, but ships do not need locks to travel the Detroit and St. Clair rivers between Lake Erie and Lake Huron, or the Straits of Mackinac between Lake Huron and Lake Michigan.

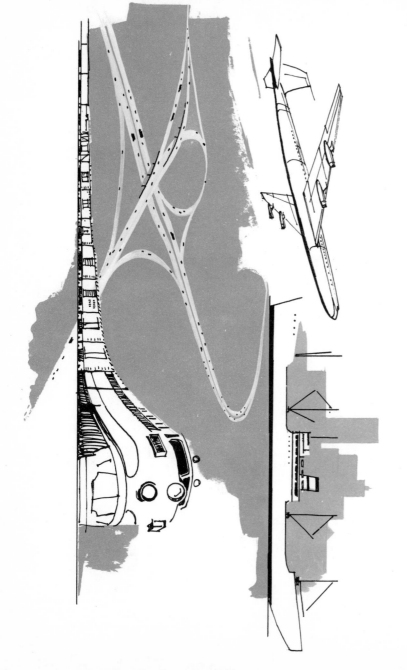

The New York State Barge Canal System connects Lakes Erie and Ontario with the Hudson River and the Atlantic Coast, while the Illinois Waterway connects Lake Michigan with the Mississippi River and the Gulf of Mexico.

The huge quantities of freight that had to be moved during World War II increased shipping on the Great Lakes and the Ohio and Mississippi rivers, and brisk trade on these waterways has continued since the war's end. Auto ferries cross Lake Michigan at several points, and, during the summer season, many small pleasure boats use the waterways. Houseboats are especially popular on the Mississippi.

The St. Lawrence Seaway and the Great Lakes are closed to shipping for about four months each year, because of ice.

From Chicago, railroads, airlines, and truck routes radiate to all parts of the country. A fine highway system has also been developed, and if you are in a very great hurry, you can now go from Chicago to New York City in one day by way of the fast toll roads that stretch across the states between the two cities.

The People

The term "melting pot" has often been applied to the United States, because her citizens are made up of many different peoples from all over the world. The wide, level land and fertile soil of the Middlewestern States, their rich iron and coal mines, and the fine transportation attracted many people from different parts of Europe. These people, in turn, developed Mid-America's great resources and made the area one of the richest in the nation.

From the very start, there was a diversity of nationalities. The French established forts and missions along the Great Lakes and in Illinois and Indiana, which were the beginnings of such towns as Cahokia and Kaskaskia in Illinois, and Vincennes in Indiana. English fur traders entered the area from Hudson Bay and sturdy frontiersmen from the eastern colonies pushed west across the mountains.

Except for a few hardy Scotch-Irish who crossed the rugged Alleghenies from Pennsylvania, the first permanent settlers in the Ohio Valley were from the East Coast. These people came soon after the new nation was founded and the Northwest Territory established.

Settlement of the areas near the Great Lakes proceeded slowly until the completion of the Erie Canal opened them to settlers from the East. Gradually, Mid-America became the "promised land" to many peoples from European countries, who looked to the United States for better living conditions and freedom from political and religious persecution.

These people brought with them the trades and arts and skills they had learned in their own countries and the traditions they had grown up with. They came from Ireland, Germany, Finland, Poland, Scandinavia, Italy, England, and Wales to farm the fertile soil and work in the iron mines and the lumbering industry. The Scandinavians made Wisconsin and Minnesota famous as dairy states; the Swiss brought their skills in making watches and cheese. Skilled farmers and craftsmen from Holland established orchards and celery farms and tulip gardens in Michigan and founded the furniture industry in Grand Rapids.

Laborers came from all over Europe to help build canals and railroads and to work in the coal mines. As industry developed in the Midwest, the factories and mills and packing houses and automobile plants attracted immigrants from Russia, Belgium, Poland, Hungary, Czecho-

48

slovakia, Lithuania, and many other countries. Some nationalities have formed colonies in the large cities, such as Chinatown and Little Poland in Chicago, and keep alive their own customs and traditions.

The original inhabitants of the Middlewestern States, the Indians, have not fared so well as the immigrants. As the white man penetrated deeper and deeper into the lands of the Indian, he pushed the Indians farther and farther north and west. Now few Indians live in Illinois and Indiana and Ohio.

There are many more in the three northern states, over 30,000 in fact, living mostly on reservations or in Indian communities. Many of them hunt and fish and gather wild rice and blueberries, much as their ancestors did. Chippewas in the North Woods country often act as guides for sportsmen.

The Arts

The French *voyageurs* sang chanteys, or boat songs, as they paddled their canoes along the waterways of Mid-America. Later, the lumber-jacks' lusty songs and the "tall tales" of Paul Bunyan and other legend-ary figures helped to develop the folklore of the Great Lakes states.

As immigrants arrived from Europe, they brought their own folk music and dances and their understanding and love for the old masters in music and art. Some of Mid-America's numerous symphony orches-tras and art museums are world famous. During the summer season, many of the cities have open-air symphonic and operatic concerts, while nearly every small town has its orchestra or band concerts in the local bandstand. In the cities, numerous art galleries exhibit the work of local and world-renowned artists.

Following the log-cabin days, the architecture of the Midwest was largely copied from that of Europe. A new type of architecture was developed in Chicago, however, with the building of the first skyscraper, after the city's great fire of 1871. Mid-America's architects had to learn to design fireproof buildings that could rise many stories into the air without toppling over. Then Frank Lloyd Wright's revolutionary ideas introduced a new architectural trend in skyscrapers, houses, churches, and other buildings. Wright's designs were based on his belief that lines should be kept simple and the building made to fit its surroundings. He believed, too, that the function of the building was important to its design.

The Midwest gave many great writers to the world, among them Hamlin Garland, Zona Gale, Edna Ferber, Thornton Wilder, Ernest Hemingway, and Sinclair Lewis, who was the first American author to receive the Nobel Prize in literature. Vachel Lindsay wrote poems to be chanted, and tramped about the countryside, reciting poetry for his supper. Carl Sandburg wrote poetry about Chicago and about Mid-America's rural life. His books about Abraham Lincoln, although they are in prose, are so beautifully written that they sound like poetry.

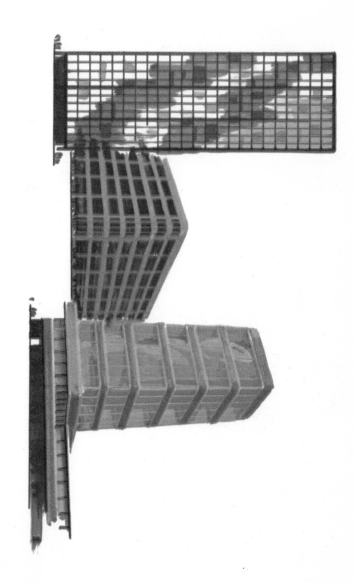

James Whitcomb Riley, with his *Little Orphant Annie* and *Book of Joyous Children*, has always been a favorite with boys and girls. So has Eugene Field, whose many poems include *Little Boy Blue*, *Wynken, Blynken, and Nod*, and *The Duel* of the gingham dog and the calico cat. Field was born in Missouri but did much of his writing in Chicago, and a monument has been erected there in his memory. Frank Baum was another author who worked in Chicago, though he came from New York. And who doesn't know his *Wonderful Wizard of Oz* and other "Oz" books!

Laura Ingalls Wilder's stories about Midwest pioneer life — *Little House in the Big Woods*, *Little House on the Prairie*, and others — are well loved, as are Annie Fellows Johnston's *Little Colonel* series.

One of the nation's most beloved poets, Henry Wadsworth Longfellow, wrote a famous poem about the Indians of the Lakes region, *The Song of Hiawatha*. Longfellow obtained much of his information about the Indians from books written by Henry Rowe Schoolcraft, the first Indian agent at Sault Ste. Marie, Michigan.

Education and Research

When Congress established the Northwest Territory and set aside one section of land in each township for schools, education in the Midwest got off to a good start. But there were few books available until William H. McGuffey, back in the 1830's, wrote a series of readers for the elementary schools. His books were soon used in schools all over the country and are still famous.

Each state now has a fine state university and other state educational institutions, as well as such privately endowed institutions as the University of Chicago and Northwestern University. Some of the state institutions helped to pioneer college agricultural departments and other vocational courses.

Mid-America has also been a pioneer in nuclear research. From the time that the first atomic furnace, or nuclear reactor, was built with great secrecy on the campus of the University of Chicago, nuclear research has gone on at the Argonne National Laboratory and in university laboratories. This research is resulting in the development of many peacetime uses of atomic energy. One of the greatest is the atomic power plants that are being set up in the Midwest and elsewhere to generate electricity.

Things to think about

What natural resources are found in the Midwest? How are they used?

How do the Great Lakes and other waterways aid industry?

Why are there so many manufacturing "capitals" in the Midwest? What are these industries?

Why is the Lakes region considered the "hub" of the nation's transportation system?

How have people from many countries contributed skills and culture to the Middlewestern States?

Lakelands enchantment

Thousands of sparkling lakes, teeming with fish, beckon us, and the North Woods country, filled with wildlife, listens for our coming. Wide, beautiful highways unwind ahead of us through the prairies and along the shores of the Great Lakes. White, sandy beaches and blue water invite us to stop for a dip and a frolic in the sand. Cool trails and bridle paths urge us into the mysterious depths of the forest. Silvery streams and flashing waterfalls spread their beauty before us, and caves filled with wonders await our exploration.

Yesterday's Charm

The vigorous, colorful past of Mid-America is still alive in the Indian mounds and historic memorials found throughout the Midwest. Wisconsin's Aztalán Mound Park contains earthworks on both banks of the Crawfish River and ceremonial and burial mounds from which pottery,

54

human bones, shells, copper artifacts, and other Indian relics have been recovered.

The Dickson Mound, on a high bluff overlooking the Spoon and Illinois rivers in Illinois, was originally a crescent-shaped mound, 550 feet long and 35 feet high. A museum has been built over it, showing more than two hundred skeletons with the clay vessels, weapons, tools, and other artifacts that were buried with them long ago. The Cahokia Group, near East St. Louis, contains many large and small mounds, including one called the Monks' Mound, which is said to be the largest earthwork in the world.

Ohio's Serpent Effigy Mound is in the form of a huge snake 1,330 feet long, with an egg in its mouth. A large group of mounds along the Scioto River in Ohio is preserved in the Mound City Group National Monument. There are many other interesting Indian mounds in the Midwest, such as Indiana's Angel Mounds, that are important archaeological sites.

Ohio's Schoenbrunn Village, in Schoenbrunn Memorial State Park, is a reconstruction of the early mission-village in Ohio founded by Moravian missionaries and a group of Christian Indians. The original village was burned, but the present village of log cabins, church, and schoolhouse has been rebuilt around the charred remains of one of the original buildings. Zoar Village, also in Ohio, contains five houses of an old German religious society; one of the buildings exhibits furniture, pottery, musical instruments, and records of the society.

Little Norway, one of the many historical sites in Wisconsin, is composed of a group of reconstructed farm buildings, showing how the Norwegian settlers of the 1850's lived. The Villa Louis, near Prairie Du Chien, is the restored 1843 mansion of a French millionaire fur trader; many of the mansion's original furnishings and some of the gowns that belonged to the ladies of the house are on display.

The days of Wisconsin's lumbering industry are represented by Eau Claire's Paul Bunyan Camp, with the tools and personal belongings of the lumberjacks, and the Logging Museum at Hayward, where log-rolling demonstrations are often staged. Also at Hayward is a Chippewa Indian village. Minnesota has Lumbertown, U.S.A., a replica of an 1870 lumber town, near Brainerd.

Two of the great historic spots in Michigan are the Mackinac area, between Lake Michigan and Lake Huron, and the Ford Museum and Greenfield Village at Dearborn, near Detroit. Mackinaw City, on the Lower Peninsula, and St. Ignace, on the Upper Peninsula, are now joined by the magnificent Mackinac Bridge, which spans the Straits of Mackinac. Father Marquette is buried at St. Ignace, site of the mission he founded in 1671. A ferry goes east from here to Mackinac Island, where horse-drawn carriages and bicycles are the only vehicles allowed. On this island are the old Mission Church, the Astor Fur House, and the reconstruction of Fort Mackinac, originally built in 1780.

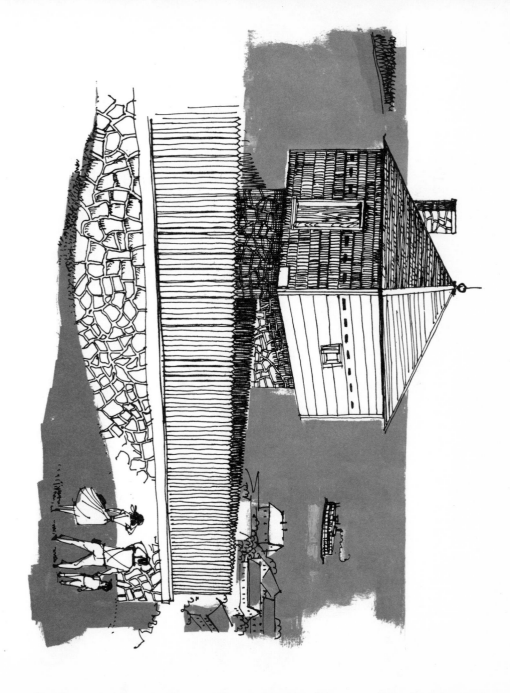

57

In Greenfield Village, Henry Ford conceived the wonderful idea of bringing together in one place nearly a hundred of the historical buildings of the nation. Some are reproductions of the originals, and some are the buildings themselves, moved from their original locations. Here are Thomas Edison's laboratory and other buildings from Menlo Park, New Jersey; the Wright home, where Orville Wright was born, and the cycle shop where the Wright Brothers produced some of the parts for their first successful airplane; the machine shop where Henry Ford finished his first horseless carriage, using bicycle wheels, plumbing pipe, and other equipment that he gathered together or made himself.

Just north of the Village Green, is a lagoon in imitation of the Suwannee River, and floating on it is the stern-wheeler *Suwannee*, which is kept in operating condition and sometimes used by the pupils who attend the several schools in the Village. Rides in horse-drawn carriages are available in the summer, as are sleigh rides in the winter.

Adjoining Greenfield Village is the Ford Museum, a huge fourteen-acre building with thousands of historical exhibits. Great halls contain displays of agriculture, crafts, transportation, and other subjects. The transportation display includes huge exhibits of automobiles and railroad locomotives. The Street of Early American Shops has the Candlemaker's Shop, the Gun and Locksmith Shop, and twenty others. The entrance to the museum is a replica of Philadelphia's Independence Hall.

Indiana's Spring Mill State Park has a reconstructed pioneer village with cabins and shops, a post office, and a grist mill powered by a water wheel.

Starved Rock and other state parks in Illinois commemorate historic forts and settlements. Galena, "the town that time forgot," contains many old buildings, including the home of Ulysses S. Grant; Nauvoo preserves the home of the Mormon leader, Joseph Smith, and other historic buildings.

Lincoln Lands

Memorials to Abraham Lincoln and his family overshadow all others in Indiana and Illinois. The Lincoln State Park, northeast of Evansville, Indiana, preserves the cabin site and much of the Indiana farm where Lincoln spent his boyhood. Nearby, in the Nancy Hanks Lincoln State Memorial, Lincoln's mother is buried. South, at the edge of Rockport, Lincoln Village is composed of the restored cabins of some of Lincoln's relatives and friends and the office where he borrowed his first law books.

59

The most remarkable memorial to Lincoln is New Salem Village, restored exactly as it was when he lived there as a young man in the 1830's. The cabins are furnished just as they were then, with such articles as cord beds, spinning wheels, and candle molds. Some of them have old-fashioned flower and vegetable gardens. The shops display the same kind of things they had for sale in the early 1800's. The Rutledge tavern is here, and the store that Lincoln once owned with William H. Berry. The Village is about twenty miles northwest of Springfield.

A handsome bridge now spans the Wabash River at Vincennes where Lincoln and his family first crossed the river into Illinois, to make it the "Land of Lincoln." The Lincoln National Memorial Highway follows the route that the Lincoln family took, and the Lincoln Trail Monument, a bronze "covered wagon," marks the spot where they entered the state. Throughout the state are memories of Lincoln and his family.

State parks mark the sites of the family's first home in Illinois, near Decatur, and the last home of Lincoln's parents, near Charleston. Numerous courthouses bear testimony that Abe Lincoln practiced law there; other places are remembered because in them Lincoln and Stephen Douglas carried on their famous debates over slavery during their campaigns for the United States Senate. The only house that Lincoln ever owned, now a state memorial, is at Springfield. In that city's Oak Ridge Cemetery is the Lincoln Tomb, containing the bodies of Lincoln, his wife, and three of their four sons.

National Monuments

There are four national monuments in the Middlewestern States, all of them largely historical. In addition to Pipestone, Minnesota has Grand Portage, containing a nine-mile Indian and French portage, as well as a reconstructed fur depot and stockade, now a museum. The Mound City Group National Monument and Perry's Victory and International Peace Memorial are in Ohio. The memorial, which is on South Bass Island in Lake Erie, commemorates the victory of Commodore Oliver Hazard Perry over the British in the War of 1812, and also celebrates the long peace between the United States and Canada.

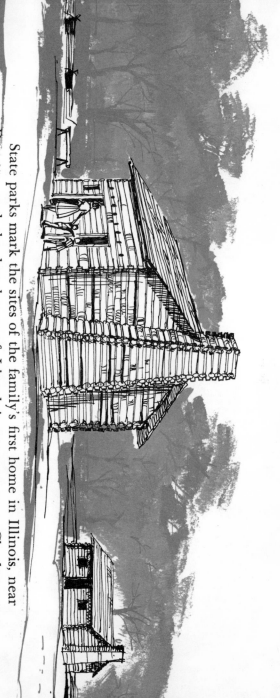

Isle Royale National Park

Isle Royale is the only national park in the Middlewestern States. It consists of a large island in Lake Superior and is one of the few real wilderness areas left in the United States. There are no roads through the deep forests and bogs that cover the island, and travel is by boat or afoot. There are convenient little inlets along the shore where boats can dock, and foot trails criss-cross the island. Moose, beaver, and other interesting wildlife live on Isle Royale, and the lakes and streams abound with fish. A government-operated passenger boat, *Ranger III*, runs between Houghton, Michigan, and Rock Harbor Lodge. There is also a lodge on Washington Harbor, at the other end of the island, and numerous lakeside campgrounds are located in convenient spots.

62

Wildlife

The North Woods country is noted for wildlife. Big-game hunting is allowed in season in many areas. Moose, deer, and bear are plentiful, and various smaller animals, such as beavers, raccoons, bobcats, foxes, rabbits, and squirrels, may be seen, especially if you are a pretty good woodsman and know how to be very quiet. Deer, to a lesser extent, and many of the smaller animals are also found in the three more southern Middlewestern States. The lakes and streams attract many waterfowls and wading birds, since the area is on a great north-south flyway; many songbirds are found throughout the Lakes region.

63

Scenery and Recreation

The thousands of lakes and streams, waterfalls, deep woods, caves, and hills of the Midwest offer scenery and recreation that is unsurpassed. Boating, water-skiing, fishing, hiking, and riding are some of the summer sports, while winter brings skating, skiing, and ice fishing.

All of the states of the Lakes region have beautiful state parks; many of them in Illinois, Indiana, and Ohio have fine lodges and other overnight accommodations, as well as campgrounds. The national forests in the northern states also have lodges, resorts, and campgrounds, and the North Woods offer wilderness adventure, too. Superior National Forest in Minnesota is a huge wilderness playground that joins the famous Quetico Provincial Park, in Canada.

Things to think about

In what ways has some of the historical charm of the Lakes region been preserved?

How has the memory of Abraham Lincoln been kept alive in this region?

Describe and explain why there is such a wide range of recreation and enjoyment to be found in the Lakes region.

In what ways has Henry Ford given so much to the people of the Midwest and to all Americans?

65

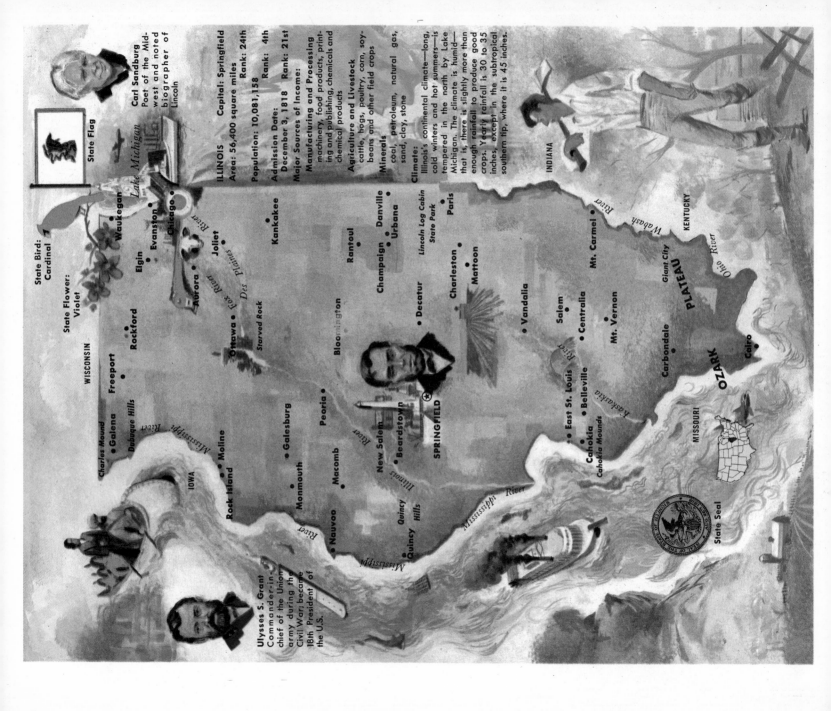

State Bird: Cardinal

State Flower: Violet

State Flag

Lake Michigan

Carl Sandburg Poet of the Midwest and noted biographer of Lincoln

ILLINOIS Capital: Springfield
Area: 56,400 square miles
Rank: 24th

Population: 10,081,158 Rank: 4th

Admission Date:
December 3, 1818 Rank: 21st

Major Sources of Income:
Manufacturing and Processing: machinery, food products, printing and publishing, chemicals and chemical products

Agriculture and Livestock:
cattle, hogs, poultry, corn, soybeans and other field crops

Minerals:
coal, petroleum, natural gas, sand, clay, stone

Climate:
Illinois's continental climate—long, cold winters and hot summers—is tempered in the north by Lake Michigan. The climate is humid, that is, there is slightly more than enough rainfall to produce good crops. Yearly rainfall is 30 to 35 inches, except in the subtropical southern tip, where it is 45 inches.

INDIANA

KENTUCKY

Wabash River

Ohio River

Giant City

PLATEAU

OZARK

Cairo

MISSOURI

State Seal

WISCONSIN

Charles Mound
Galena
Dubuque Hills
Freeport
Rockford

IOWA

Mississippi River

Moline
Rock Island
Monmouth
Macomb
Nauvoo
Quincy
Quincy Hills

Galesburg
Peoria

Mississippi River

Illinois River

Waukegan
Elgin
Evanston
Chicago
Aurora
Joliet

Fox River
Des Plaines River

Starved Rock
Ottawa

Bloomington

New Salem
Beardstown
SPRINGFIELD

Decatur

Champaign
Urbana
Rantoul
Danville

Kankakee

Lincoln Log Cabin State Park
Paris

Charleston
Mattoon

Vandalia
Salem
Centralia
Mt. Vernon

Carbondale

Kaskaskia River

East St. Louis
Belleville
Cahokia
Cahokia Mounds

Ulysses S. Grant Commander-in-chief of the Union army during the Civil War; became 18th President of the U.S.

Illinois, "the Land of Lincoln," is also the crossroads of the nation. Even before the white man came, the area was criss-crossed with Indian trails; now it is the hub of highways, railroads, and airlines. The heart of the nation's great inland waterways system, Illinois is largely surrounded by navigable water, with Lake Michigan on the northeast, the Wabash River on the southeast, the Ohio on the south, and the Mississippi on the west.

Although early settlers nicknamed Illinois the "Prairie State," it does not have nearly as much prairie as some of the more western states. In pioneer days, much of Illinois was covered with forests, but its prairie lands were the first that the settlers from the east had ever seen.

Important Whens and Whats in the Making of Illinois

1673 French fur trader, Louis Jolliet and Jesuit priest, Jacques Marquette are the first white travelers to arrive in Illinois country.

1763 France gives up holdings east of the Mississippi, including Illinois land, to England after final defeat in the French and Indian War.

1778 After the revolt of the 13 colonies in the East, George Rogers Clark captures British holdings in the Illinois region; Virginia Assembly makes Illinois a county of Virginia.

1784 Virginia cedes her claim to Illinois lands to the federal government.

1787 The great Northwest Territory, including Illinois country, is created.

1800 The Illinois region is included in the newly created Indiana Territory.

1809 Illinois, the western part of Indiana Territory, becomes a separate Territory which includes land that will later become Wisconsin, Michigan and part of Minnesota.

1818 Illinois is admitted to the Union as the 21st state.

Illinois does not lack hills. The Mississippi and Illinois rivers frequently flow between high limestone bluffs, of which Starved Rock, now a state park, is a good example. And the rocky hills and spires of the northwest corner, as well as the Ozark Mountains that spill across the southern end from Missouri, offer striking contrast to the level stretches between. The rock formations in Giant City State Park look as though a giant had been tumbling them about.

The extreme southern tip of Illinois, where the Ohio River empties into the Mississippi, is often called "Egypt" because of its warm, subtropical climate and its fine fields of cotton. Cairo is "Egypt's" main city.

Between here and the state's industrial north are millions of acres of soybeans, corn, wheat, hay, and other grain and fodder crops, as well as vegetables and fruits. Illinois leads the nation in the production of soybeans and competes with Iowa for the title of Corn King. Much of the grain and hay is fed to livestock — cattle, sheep, hogs, and horses — and to poultry. The Chicago Board of Trade is the major grain market in the country.

Chicago is the nation's greatest railroad center. The state's heaviest concentration of industry is also centered in Chicago and Cook County. Three of the largest steel mills in the nation are in the Chicago Metropolitan Area.

Situated at the southern tip of Lake Michigan, Chicago has done much to preserve and beautify her lakefront. Wide bathing beaches extend for miles along the shore. Towns north of Chicago have also preserved their beaches, and the Illinois Beach State Park adds another three and a half miles of public beach.

Along Chicago's Lake Shore Drive are parks and museums and entertainment facilities. At 59th Street, the Museum of Science and Industry contains a German submarine, a coal mine, one of the first diesel-powered trains, an astronaut's space suit, and electronic, atomic, and hundreds of other scientific exhibits. Farther north are the giant stadium called Soldier Field, the Field Museum of Natural History, Shedd Aquarium, Adler Planetarium, and McCormick Place, a huge exposition hall where all sorts of fairs and shows are held. Grant Park contains the lovely Buckingham Fountain and the bandshell where thousands of people hear open-air concerts during the summer season.

Just west of the Drive is the city's fabulous Loop, with its tall skyscrapers and famous stores. West of the city, Brookfield Zoo confines its animals in areas resembling their natural habitats, surrounded by moats. Still farther west, Morton's Arboretum contains trees and shrubs from all parts of the world.

Chicago boasts two big-league baseball teams — the White Sox, of the American League, and the Cubs, in the National League.

69

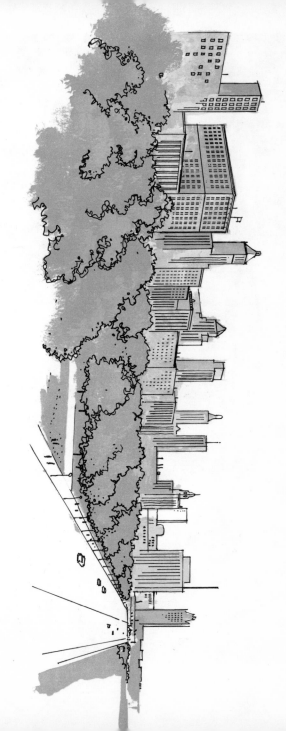

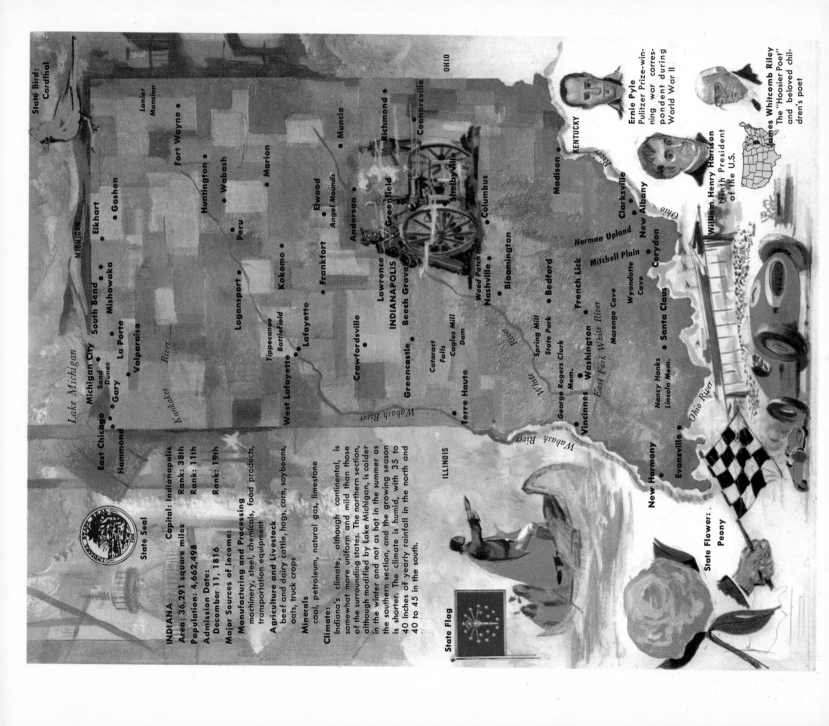

State Bird: Cardinal

State Seal

INDIANA

Capital: Indianapolis

Area: 36,291 square miles — Rank: 38th
Population: 4,662,498 — Rank: 11th

Admission Date:
December 11, 1816 — Rank: 19th

Major Sources of Income:

Manufacturing and Processing
machinery, steel, chemicals, food products, transportation equipment

Agriculture and Livestock
beef and dairy cattle, hogs, corn, soybeans, oats, truck crops

Minerals
coal, petroleum, natural gas, limestone

Climate:
Indiana's climate, although continental, is somewhat more uniform and mild than those of the surrounding states. The northern section, although modified by Lake Michigan, is colder in the winter and not as hot in the summer as the southern section, and the growing season is shorter. The climate is humid, with 35 to 40 inches of yearly rainfall in the north and 40 to 45 in the south.

State Flag

State Flower: Peony

MICHIGAN

Lake Michigan

OHIO

KENTUCKY

ILLINOIS

Lanier Mansion

Fort Wayne

Huntington
Wabash
Marion
Peru
Goshen
Elkhart
South Bend
Mishawaka
La Porte
Michigan City
Sand Dunes
Gary
Valparaiso
East Chicago
Hammond

Kankakee River

Logansport
Kokomo
Elwood
Frankfort
Anderson
Muncie
Angel Mounds
Richmond
Connersville
Shelbyville
Greenfield
Lawrence
INDIANAPOLIS
Beech Grove
Lafayette
West Lafayette
Tippecanoe Battlefield
Crawfordsville
Greencastle
Cataract Falls
Eagles Mill Dam
Terre Haute

Columbus
Norman Upland
Bloomington
Nashville
Weed Patch Hill
Mitchell Plain
Bedford
Spring Mill State Park
French Lick
Washington
George Rogers Clark Mem.
Vincennes
Nancy Hanks Lincoln Mem.
New Harmony
Evansville
Marengo Cave
Wyandotte Cave
East Fork White River
Corydon
New Albany
Clarksville
Madison
Santa Claus

White River

Wabash River

Ohio River

William Henry Harrison Ninth President of the U.S.

Ernie Pyle Pulitzer Prize-winning war correspondent during World War II

James Whitcomb Riley The "Hoosier Poet" and beloved children's poet

Indiana

Although most parts of Indiana are still chiefly agricultural, industry exceeds agriculture in dollar value. Heavy industry is concentrated largely along the lake front from Gary north and west to Chicago. Indiana's few miles of remaining lake front and her system of state parks preserve outstanding scenic areas and historic sites.

Important Whens and Whats in the Making of Indiana

1675 Father Marquette crosses the dunes of Lake Michigan and soon afterward, La Salle follows the St. Joseph and Kankakee rivers into what is now Indiana.

1735 The French establish one of the first permanent trading posts at Fort Vincennes.

1763 The British take over the region after their victory in the French and Indian War.

1779 During the American Revolution, General George Rogers Clark captures Vincennes from the British.

1784 The Northwest Territory, including the Indiana region is created after the Virginia Assembly cedes her claims to this land to the federal government.

1800 The Indiana territory is created from the Northwest Territory.

1809 The Indiana territory is divided; the western part is named the Illinois Territory.

1811 General William Henry Harrison's defeat of Tecumseh in the battle of Tippecanoe checks Indian warfare in the region.

1816 Indiana is admitted to the Union as the 19th state.

71

A beautiful region of shifting sand dunes, wooded hills, and small lakes and ponds lies along the lake shore between Gary and Michigan City. Such plants as the arctic jack pine, brought here thousands of years ago by the glaciers, and fragile orchids from subtropical swamps are found growing together, bringing scientists from all over the world to study the area. For years a battle has been waged between encroaching industrial interests and citizens who wish to preserve the beauty and scientific values of the Dunes.

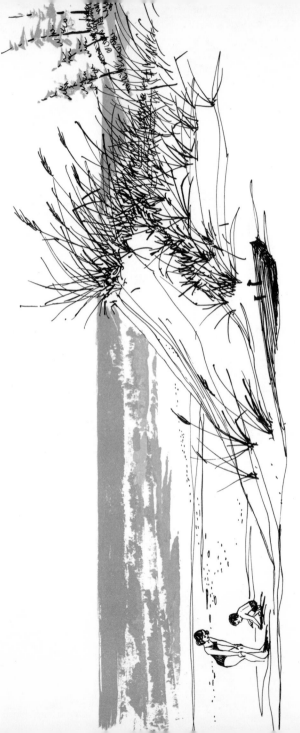

Once covered by forests, Indiana is generally level, except for moraines laid down by the glaciers and the scenic hill country in the south. The state has the Ohio River as a boundary on the south, the Wabash on the southwest, and Lake Michigan on the northwest.

Her heavy industries consist of oil refineries, steel mills, and limestone quarries and mills. Interesting light industries are the processing of peppermint and spearmint and the canning of tomatoes grown in the state. Corn is Indiana's major crop, followed by winter wheat, oats, soybeans, and truck farming. Tobacco is grown in the south.

Indianapolis, the state's capital, is also its largest city. In addition to the museums, hospitals, and other institutions usually found in a large city, the Memorial Day "500" race at Indianapolis' Motor Speedway has become world famous. Indianapolis has several institutions of special interest to children. One is the Children's Museum, which has twenty-four rooms of exhibits; another is the James Whitcomb Riley Hospital for Children, a unit of the Indiana University Medical Center, with art-glass windows and wall decorations that illustrate Riley's poems. At Greenfield is Riley's home, furnished just as it was when Riley lived in it.

Wyandotte Cave, in the southern Indiana hills, contains many beautiful formations, including rare helicites. It has twenty-three miles of underground trails and is believed to be the third largest cave in the United States. Marengo Cave, in the same vicinity, also has some beautiful formations. Southwest of here, near the Nancy Hanks Lincoln State Memorial, is the town of Santa Claus, where thousands of letters are sent at Christmas to be postmarked.

In the northwestern corner of the state, at Michigan City, are the International Friendship Gardens, in which there is a constant display of flowers from plants contributed from countries all over the world.

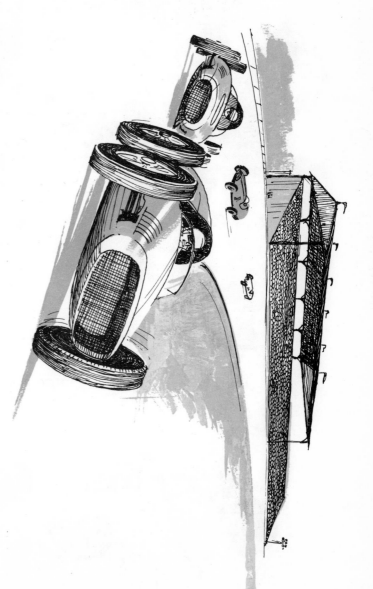

State Seal

WISCONSIN

Charles A. Lindbergh
Made the first non-stop solo flight from New York to Paris

Henry Ford
Pioneer auto manufacturer; born in Greenfield Village

Ring Lardner
Short story writer of the sports world; born in Niles

MICHIGAN
Area: 58,216 square miles
Population: 7,823,194
Admission Date: January 26, 1837
Major Sources of Income:
Manufacturing and Processing
motor vehicles, machinery, chemicals, food products, furniture

Agriculture and Livestock
fruits and vegetables, grains, dairy cattle, poultry

Minerals
iron ore, salt, peat, gypsum, sand, stone, gravel

Tourist Expenditures

Capital: Lansing   Rank: 23rd
   Rank: 7th
   Rank: 26th

Climate:
The continental climate of Michigan's Lower Peninsula is considerably modified by its nearness to the Great Lakes. The Upper Peninsula has long, severe winters. The growing season ranges from 90 to 170 days and the yearly rainfall from 25 to 35 inches.

State Flag

State Bird:
Robin

State Flower:
Apple Blossom

Lake Superior

Keweenaw Peninsula
Copper Range
Porcupine Mts.
Gogebic Range
Ironwood
Pt. Abbaye
Keweenaw Bay
Huron Mts.
Lake Michigamme
Marquette
Ishpeming
Iron River
Menominee Range
Iron Mountain
Menominee
Escanaba
Big Bay de Noc
Whitefish River
Munising
Pictured Rocks
Manistique
Manistique Lake
Tahquamenon Falls
Whitefish Pt.
Whitefish Bay
Soo Locks
Sault Ste. Marie
CANADA
Drummond I.
Mackinac I.
St. Ignace
Straits of Mackinac
Bois Blanc I.
Garden I.
High I.
Little Beaver I.
Beaver I.
BEAVER ISLANDS

Lake Huron
Long Lake
North Pt.
Thunder Bay
Alpena
Hubbard Lake
Cheboygan
Petoskey
Charlevoix
Houghton Lake
Grand Traverse Bay
Traverse City
Pt. Betsie
Interlochen
Cadillac
Pere Marquette River
Big Rapids
Muskegon River
Grand River
Big Sable Pt.
Ludington
Little Sable Pt.
Muskegon
Grand Rapids
Holland
Benton Harbor
St. Joseph
Bear Cave
Niles
INDIANA
Kalamazoo River
Kalamazoo
Battle Creek
Jackson
Sturgis
Grand River
Mt. Pleasant
Midland
Alma
LANSING
Irish Hills
Ann Arbor
Ypsilanti
Flint
Saginaw
Saginaw Bay
Pte. Aux Barques
Port Huron
Lake St. Clair
Detroit
Dearborn
Greenfield Village
OHIO
Detroit River
Lake Erie

Lake Michigan

Michigan, almost surrounded by four of the five Great Lakes and with thousands of smaller lakes within her borders, is truly a "Water Wonderland." The state is composed of two great peninsulas, the Upper and the Lower. The Lower Peninsula is in the form of a mitten, with Lake Huron on the north and east, Lake Erie on the southeast, and Lake Michigan on the west. Saginaw Bay makes the thumb, and this mitten also has a little finger—formed by Grand Traverse Bay, off Lake Michigan. The Upper Peninsula has Lake Superior on the north and Lakes Michigan and Huron on the south. The two peninsulas were separated by the water of the Straits of Mackinac until the great Mackinac Bridge was completed in 1957.

Important Whens and Whats in the Making of Michigan

1618-1669 French explorers, Brulé, Nicolet, Marquette, Jolliet and others, enter the Michigan region; establish military, missionary and trading posts.

1763 The victorious British take over Michigan lands after the bloody French and Indian War.

1787 The Michigan region is included in the Northwest Territory.

1796 England gives up Detroit and Fort Michilimackinac to the United States.

1805 Michigan becomes a separate Territory.

1813 Michigan is in British hands during the War of 1812 until American forces defeat the British in the battle of Lake Erie and the battle of the Thames, and American control of the Northwest is restored.

1837 Michigan is admitted to the Union as the 26th state.

The copper-rich Keweenaw Peninsula extends northward into Lake Superior, and Isle Royale lies across the lake to the northwest. On each side of the Keweenaw Peninsula are Michigan's great iron mines. Another of the state's important resources is natural gas, of which there are twelve large fields, located in central Michigan. The state also claims the largest limestone quarries in the world and the largest fresh-fruit auction, located at Benton Harbor, in the heart of the fruit belt that extends along the east shore of Lake Michigan.

Magnificent tulips are grown in western Michigan, an industry which was started by immigrants from the Netherlands and has been carried on by their descendants. A four-day tulip festival is held at Holland in May of each year, when the people dress in Dutch costumes, and millions of tulip blossoms are on display along the city streets and surrounding countryside. Colorful folk dances are performed in the streets, and wooden shoes are in evidence everywhere.

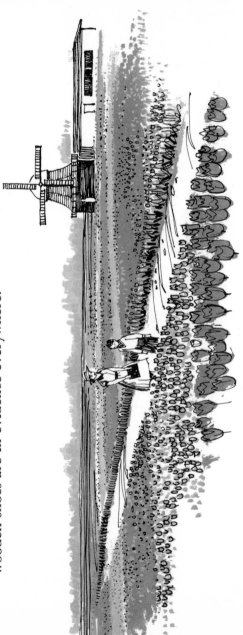

Tourism in Michigan vies with the manufacture of automobiles as the state's leading industry. Summer vacationers are attracted by the cool North Woods and the many lakes with bathing beaches. Sportsmen like the opportunities for fishing in the lakes and streams and hunting during the season. Winter sports are important, too, with fine ski runs at such points as Boyne Mountain, Pine Mountain, and Porcupine Mountains State Park.

A great favorite with tourists is the Mackinac area, with its scenic and historical attractions. North from here on the Upper Peninsula, across Whitefish Bay on Lake Superior, is Tahquamenon Falls State Park. Westward, near Munising, are the colorful Pictured Rocks. All of this area is the land of Longfellow's legendary Hiawatha. Lake Superior is the "Big-Sea-Water" of the poem, and Hiawatha's birch-bark canoe glided along the Tahquamenon River.

The sand dunes along Lake Michigan are another popular tourist attraction. Dunesmobiles take visitors from Glen Haven to the famous Sleeping Bear Dune and to other points along the dunes for superb views of Lake Michigan and Glen Lake.

Detroit, Michigan's largest city, is not only the automobile capital of the world—it also has a leading American League baseball team, the Tigers.

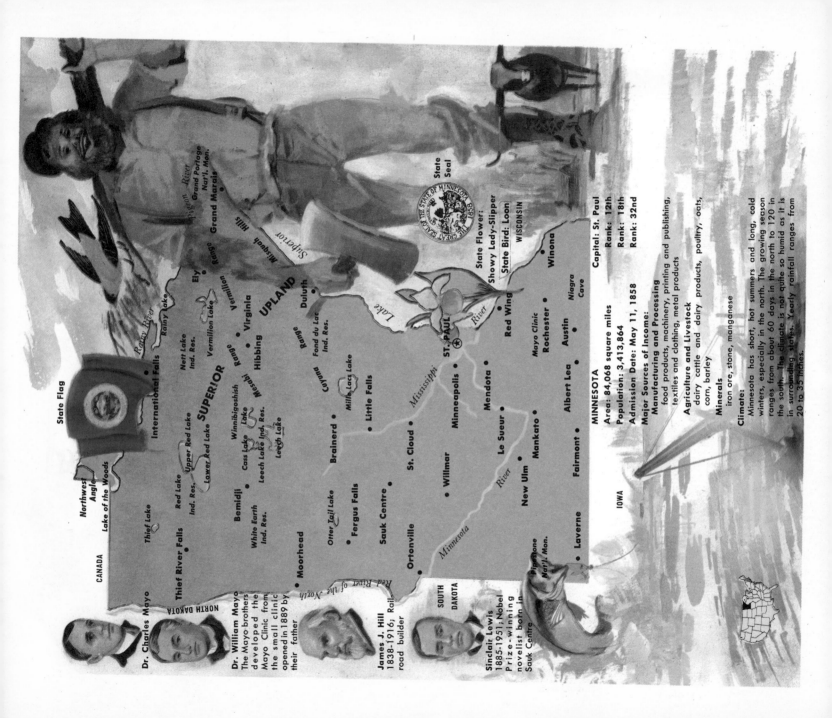

State Flag

Northwest Angle
Lake of the Woods

CANADA

State Seal

State Flower:
Showy Lady-Slipper
State Bird: **Loon**

WISCONSIN

Winona

MINNESOTA

Area: 84,068 square miles   Rank: 12th
Population: 3,413,864   Rank: 18th
Admission Date: May 11, 1858   Rank: 32nd

Major Sources of Income:

  Manufacturing and Processing
  food products, machinery, printing and publishing, textiles and clothing, metal products

  Agriculture and Livestock
  dairy cattle and dairy products, poultry, oats, corn, barley

  Minerals
  iron ore, stone, manganese

Climate:
Minnesota has short, hot summers and long, cold winters, especially in the north. The growing season ranges from about 60 days in the north to 120 in the south. The climate is not quite so humid as it is in surrounding states. Yearly rainfall ranges from 20 to 35 inches.

Capital: St. Paul

Mississippi River
ST. PAUL
Minneapolis
Mendota
Le Sueur
Mankato
New Ulm
Fairmont
Laverne
Pipestone Nat'l. Mon.
Ortonville
Willmar
St. Cloud
Sauk Centre
Fergus Falls
Otter Tail Lake
Brainerd
Little Falls
Mille Lacs Lake
Cuyuna Range
Fond du Lac Ind. Res.
Duluth
Red Wing
Mayo Clinic Rochester
Austin
Albert Lea
Niagra Cave

IOWA

SOUTH DAKOTA
NORTH DAKOTA

Moorhead
White Earth Ind. Res.
Bemidji
Cass Lake
Leech Lake Ind. Res.
Leech Lake
Winnibigoshish Lake
Lower Red Lake
Upper Red Lake
Red Lake Ind. Res.
Thief Lake
Thief River Falls
International Falls
Rainy Lake
Rainy River
Nett Lake Ind. Res.
Ely
Vermilion Lake
Virginia
Hibbing
Mesabi Range
Vermilion
Grand Marais
Grand Portage Nat'l. Mon.
Pigeon River
Misquah Hills
Superior

SUPERIOR
UPLAND

Lake Superior

Red River of the North
Minnesota River

Dr. Charles Mayo

Dr. William Mayo
1838-1916; The Mayo brothers developed the Mayo Clinic from the small clinic opened in 1889 by their father

James J. Hill
1838-1916; Railroad builder

Sinclair Lewis
1885-1951; Nobel Prize-winning novelist born in Sauk Centre

Minnesota, self-styled "Land of 10,000 Lakes," shares with Canada some of the most magnificent wilderness in North America. The northeast corner of the state, which is a maze of lakes and streams, is called the Arrowhead Country because the long diagonal shoreline of Lake Superior on the southeast and the Canadian Border on the north form an area that is almost a perfect arrowhead. At the tip of the arrowhead, where the Pigeon River flows into Lake Superior, are the Grand Portage Indian Reservation and Grand Portage National Monument.

Important Whens and Whats in the Making of Minnesota

1659 French explorers and fur traders Radisson and Des Groseilliers, (brothers-in-law) make the first entry into the Minnesota region.

1763 After the French and Indian War, the French cede their claims to land east of the Mississippi, including part of the Minnesota region, to Great Britain.

1783 After the American Revolution, the Minnesota region goes to the United States.

1787 The Northwest Territory is created, including part of Minnesota lands.

1803 Land west of the Mississippi River becomes United States property by the Louisiana Purchase.

1823 The *Virginia*, first steamboat to travel the upper Mississippi, arrives at Fort Snelling.

1832 The source of the Mississippi River is discovered by Henry Schoolcraft in Lake Itasca.

1837 Settlement begins in Minnesota lands.

1849 Minnesota becomes a separate Territory.

1858 Minnesota is admitted to the Union as the 32nd state.

79

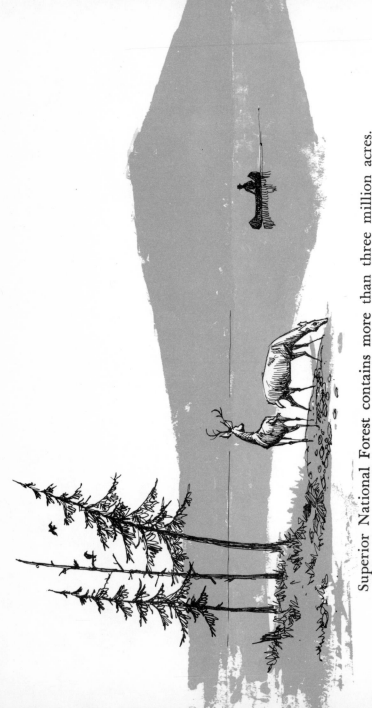

Superior National Forest contains more than three million acres. About a third of this, called the Boundary Waters Canoe Area, has been set aside as a great wilderness area, penetrated only by canoes. There are no roads, and airplanes are not allowed to land there. A paved road, called the Gunflint Trail, goes from Grand Marais to Saganaga Lake, at the edge of the wilderness area. A graveled road goes to Moose Lake, near Ely, and another one to Sawbill Lake, other "jumping-off places" into the Canoe Area.

Roads go into the Mesabi Iron Range, where visitors can view the huge, open-pit iron mines. West of here are some of the largest lakes in the state — Lake Winnibigoshish and Leech Lake, on the Leech Lake Indian Reservation, and the Upper and Lower Red Lakes on the Red Lake Reservation. Also in the area is Itasca State Park, where the Mississippi, mightiest of North America's rivers, heads up. On the Canadian border, the state shares Lake of the Woods with Canada. A corner of Minnesota, which is entirely separated from the rest of the state, juts into this huge lake, which is famous with sportsmen from all over the world. These are only a few of the lakes and rivers that gave the state the name of Minnesota, which is the Sioux Indian name for "sky-blue waters."

80

The iron ore for nearly 70 per cent of all the steel made in the United States is mined in Minnesota. Minnesota makes more butter and grows more sweet corn than any other state, and the total of all her farm products makes her fifth nationally in agriculture. Manufacturing, centered around St. Paul, Minneapolis, and other cities, is even more important than farming, and Duluth is one of the greatest ports on the Great Lakes. In the medical column, the state is famous for the Mayo Clinic, located at Rochester. Minnesota's American League baseball team is the Twins, based at Minneapolis.

In 1963 Minneapolis opened the doors of a new playhouse—the Tyrone Guthrie Theatre. Staffed by experienced actors and actresses the theatre presents a new series of plays each year that have achieved nationwide critical acclaim.

Minnesota shares her folklore and music with the whole nation. From Bemidji and Brainerd come many of the tall tales about Paul Bunyan. West of Minneapolis is Lake Minnetonka, which inspired two popular songs, Thurlow Lieurance's "By the Waters of the Minnetonka," and Charles W. Cadman's "From the Land of the Sky-Blue Water."

81

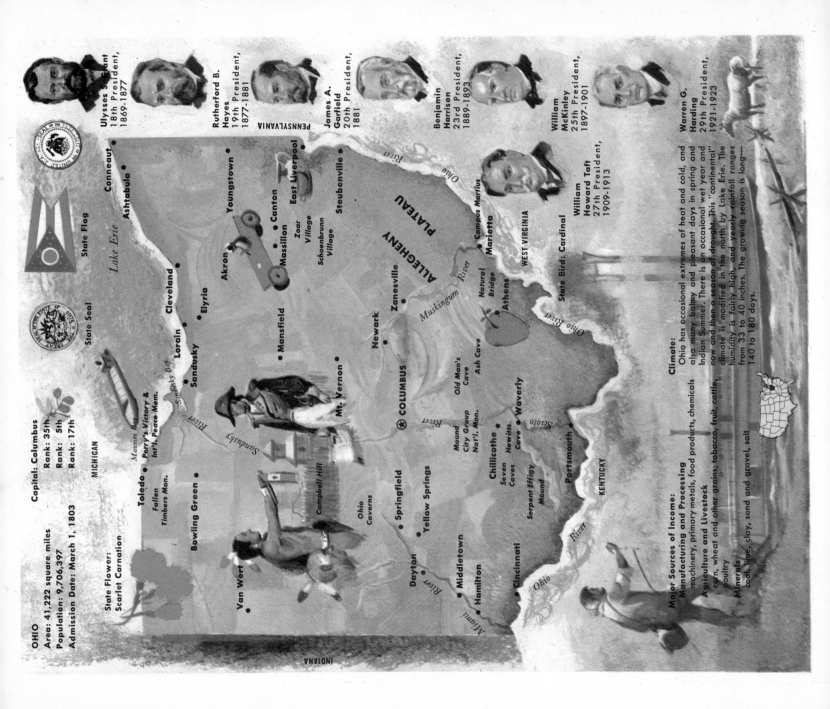

OHIO

Area: 41,222 square miles   Rank: 35th
Population: 9,706,397   Rank: 5th
Admission Date: March 1, 1803   Rank: 17th

Capital: Columbus

State Flower: Scarlet Carnation

State Seal

State Flag

SEAL OF THE UNITED STATES

GREAT SEAL OF THE STATE OF OHIO

Ulysses S. Grant
18th President,
1869-1877

Rutherford B. Hayes
19th President,
1877-1881

James A. Garfield
20th President,
1881

Benjamin Harrison
23rd President,
1889-1893

William McKinley
25th President,
1897-1901

Warren G. Harding
29th President,
1921-1923

William Howard Taft
27th President,
1909-1913

State Bird: Cardinal

MICHIGAN

PENNSYLVANIA

WEST VIRGINIA

KENTUCKY

INDIANA

Lake Erie

Conneaut

Ashtabula

Youngstown

Canton

East Liverpool

Steubenville

Massillon

Zoar Village

Schoenbrunn Village

Akron

Cleveland

Elyria

Lorain

Sandusky

Maumee Bay

Toledo

Perry's Victory & Int'l. Peace Mem.

Fallen Timbers Mon.

Bowling Green

Van Wert

Campbell Hill

Ohio Caverns

Springfield

Yellow Springs

Dayton

Middletown

Hamilton

Cincinnati

Mansfield

Mt. Vernon

COLUMBUS

Newark

Zanesville

Old Man's Cave

Ash Cave

Mound City Group Nat'l. Mon.

Chillicothe

Seven Caves

Hewitt's Cave

Serpent Effigy Mound

Waverly

Portsmouth

Natural Bridge

Athens

Marietta

Campus Martius

ALLEGHENY PLATEAU

Muskingum River

Ohio River

Scioto River

Sandusky River

Sandusky Bay

Ohio River

Miami River

Ohio River

Major Sources of Income:

Manufacturing and Processing
machinery, primary metals, food products, chemicals

Agriculture and Livestock
corn, wheat and other grains; tobacco, fruit, cattle, poultry

Minerals
coal, lime, clay, sand and gravel, salt

Climate:

Ohio has occasional extremes of heat and cold, and also many balmy and pleasant days in spring and Indian Summer. There is an occasional wet year and now and then a season of drought. This "continental" climate is modified in the north by Lake Erie. The humidity is fairly high, and yearly rainfall ranges from 33 to 40 inches. The growing season is long—140 to 180 days.

Historic Ohio was the gateway to the Northwest Territory, and it is still a sort of funnel for transportation between the north-central states and the north and central Atlantic states. Many of the settlers who came down the Ohio River or crossed New York State to Lake Erie on the Erie Canal landed on Ohio's green shores and either made their homes in her fertile valleys or pushed through them to lands beyond.

Important Whens and Whats in the Making of Ohio

1669 La Salle and a party from Montreal may have been the first white men to reach Ohio lands.

1749 British colonists build a trading post at the Miami Indian Village of Pickaivillany.

1763 Ohio country goes to the British with other French claims after the French and Indian War.

1772 Moravian missionaries and Christian Indians build a village, Schoenbrunn.

1778 During the Revolutionary War, Fort Laurens, most western post of General Washington's armies, is built as a defense outpost against the British.

1788 Marietta is settled by the Ohio Company of Berton.

1795 After American victory at the battle of Fallen Timbers, the Treaty of Greenville, signed by General Anthony Wayne and 90 Indians representing 12 tribes, fixes boundary lines between Americans and Indians; settlement spreads into the Ohio interior and westward.

1803 Ohio is admitted to the Union as the 17th state.

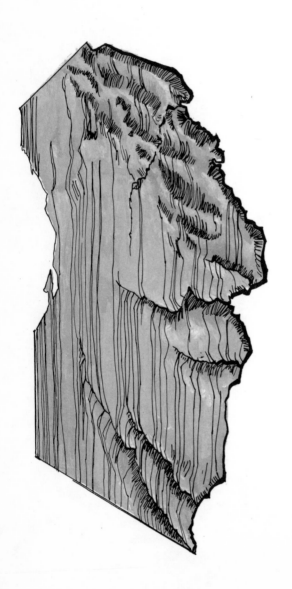

Like the other Middlewestern States, most of Ohio's borders are formed by water, with Lake Erie on the north and the Ohio River on the east and south. The state is really almost as much eastern as midwestern, for the Allegheny Plateau, a part of the Appalachian Highlands, extends across the eastern half of the state. Much of the land here is more than 1,400 feet high, and the rivers have cut deep valleys through the hills. The western half of the state is a rolling plain, part of the central lowlands. The wide valley of the Miami River is in the southwestern section, while the northwest is a flat lake plain, once the floor of a lake far larger than Lake Erie.

Ohio's strategic position as the eastern end of the Corn Belt makes the state important in agriculture and stock raising, especially hogs. Small fruits, such as grapes, apples, and peaches, grow in the areas near the lake, and tobacco is cultivated in the southwest.

Ohio has few natural lakes, but she has built many man-made ones, for flood control and for recreational purposes. She was the first state in the Union to set up conservancy districts for flood control and conservation projects. One of the first was the Muskingum District, which contains fifteen dams and eleven permanent lakes. These lakes not only control the flood waters along the Muskingum watershed, but provide recreational areas for thousands of people.

Ohio's many historical monuments, shrines, and museums also attract many visitors. The Anthony Wayne Parkway is a system of marked highways that follow the routes used by General Wayne in his campaign against the Indians. The Parkway goes from Cincinnati to Toledo and up the Maumee River Valley to Fort Wayne, Indiana, with monuments marking the sites of forts and battlefields along the way.

Eight presidents and three vice-presidents of the United States were born in Ohio, and their birthplaces and tombs have been preserved as national shrines. Another interesting spot is the "President's Half Acre," a stone-walled plot of land deeded to the President of the United States by a pioneer settler in 1838. Each succeeding president receives title to this bit of land.

There are many historic landmarks at Marietta, first permanent settlement in Ohio, which is located at the junction of the Muskingum and Ohio rivers. One of the most notable museums here is the Campus Martius, which contains many historic relics of early days and encloses the home of Rufus Putnam, original founder of the settlement.

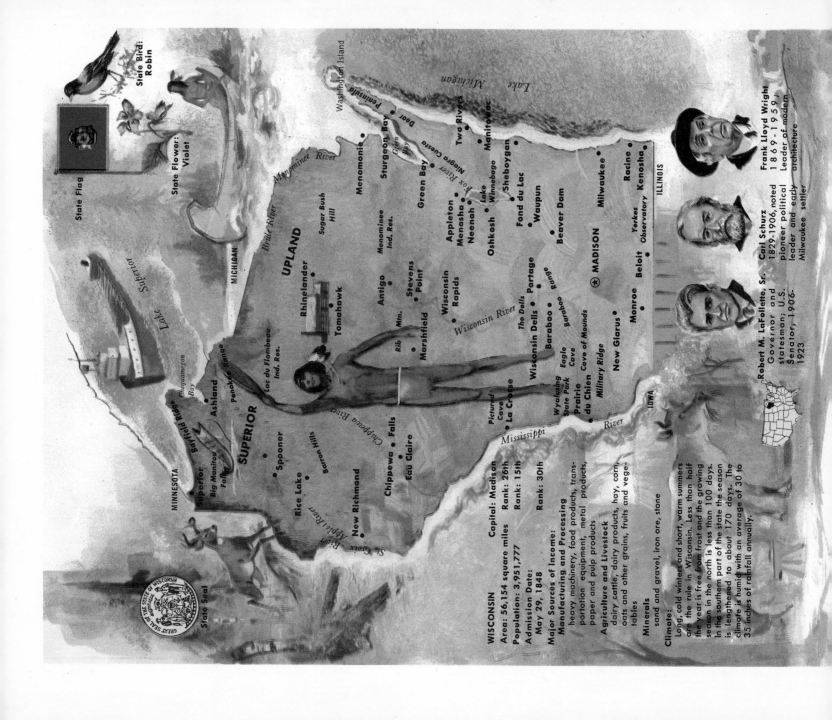

Wisconsin's claim to waterways consists of Lake Superior on the north, Lake Michigan on the east, and the Mississippi River on the west. From Madison east, the state is largely a glaciated plain, with moraines for hills. The southwestern quarter is in the hilly Driftless Area, which the ice sheets did not cover, and there are low mountains and deep forests in the north, with lakes all over the state except in the Driftless Area.

Important Whens and Whats in the Making of Wisconsin

1634   French explorer, Jean Nicolet, lands at Red Banks, the first white man to reach Wisconsin country.

1673   Jolliet and Marquette explore the Mississippi River from Prairie Du Chien to the mouth of the Arkansas River.

1763   Part of New France, Wisconsin lands become part of British colonial territory after the French and Indian War.

1764   The first permanent settlement is made at Green Bay.

1783   After the American Revolution, Wisconsin lands become part of the United States by the Treaty of Paris.

1787   Wisconsin land is included in the Northwest Territory.

1815   After the War of 1812, the last of the British leave Wisconsin.

1816   The Astor Fur Company begins operations in Wisconsin country.

1832   Black Hawk War.

1836   Wisconsin becomes a separate Territory.

1848   Wisconsin is admitted to the Union as the 30th state.

Wisconsin is justly proud of being called the "Dairy State." Number One state in the production of cheese, she is also a leader in many of the other dairy products. Although most of the agricultural produce is used to support the dairy industry, some beef cattle, sheep, hogs, horses, and poultry are raised. Tobacco is cultivated in the southern section. Some of the interesting products of the state's manufacturing plants are paper, machinery, internal combustion engines, motor vehicles, plumbing equipment, and leather goods.

With the completion of the St. Lawrence Seaway, Milwaukee, on Lake Michigan, is rapidly becoming a great world port. An important industrial center, the city has become famous for its breweries.

Tourism is a leading industry, with the state's share of North Woods, thousands of lakes for fishing, boating, and swimming, and its many other recreational facilities. Hunting is fine in the fall, and the forests' autumn foliage is beautiful then. Winter-sport fans enjoy skiing, skating, ice-boating, and ice-fishing.

88

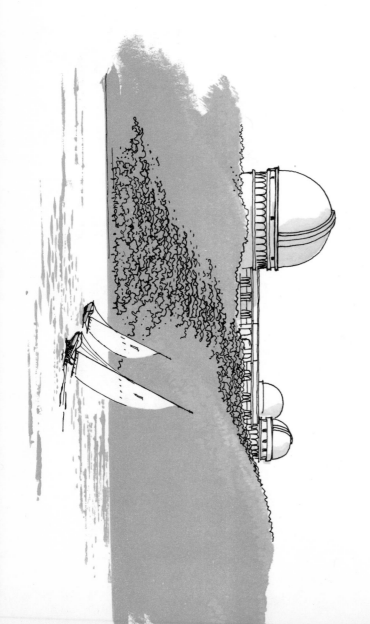

Lake Winnebago, northwest of Milwaukee, is the largest in the state. Southeast of it, the Old Wade House State Park preserves an early-day stagecoach inn. Madison, the state capital, is in an especially scenic area. Surrounded by a group of four lakes, the city is located on a narrow neck of land between two of them — Lakes Mendota and Monona. A few miles west are Little Norway, Blue Mounds State Park, Cave of Mounds, and Lost River Cave.

On the Wisconsin River, northwest of Portage, is the famous Wisconsin Dells area. Launches cruise the rugged gorges of the river, and trails follow its banks. During the summer, colorful Indian ceremonials are held nightly in an outdoor amphitheatre at Stand Rock. There are also several historic and amusement parks.

The Dalles of the St. Croix River, 200 feet deep in places, are in the Interstate Park, which is shared by Wisconsin and Minnesota. Here, too, are fantastic rock formations, and a lake with bathing beaches.

Down in the southeast corner of the state, at Williams Bay on Lake Geneva, is the University of Chicago's Yerkes Astronomical Observatory, containing one of the nation's most powerful telescopes.

Glossary

Alleghenies (ăl′ ĕ gā′nīz)   mountain ranges of the Appalachian system in the eastern United States.

artifact (är′tĭ făkt) a product of human workmanship, especially of primitive skill.

bison (bī′s'n; bī′z′n) the American buffalo.

bluff (blŭf) a part of mountains or hills which rises steeply with a broad, flat or rounded front, as a coast or at the edge of some rivers.

erosion (ē rō′zhŭn) the eating away of land by the action of water, ice, or wind.

extinct (ĕks tĭngkt′) no longer living or active; that which has died out, as an animal or plant.

flyway (flī′wā′) an established air route followed by birds that migrate.

fossil (fŏs′ĭl) any impression or trace of an animal or plant of the past that has been preserved in the earth's crust.

glaciated (glā′shĭ āt′d) the action or effect of a glacier, as erosion and relocated earth.

glacier (glā′shẽr) a field or body of ice which moves slowly down a valley from above.

gristmill (grĭst′mĭl) a mill for grinding grain.

ground sloth (ground slŏth; slôth) a slow-moving mammal which stays on the ground, found in tropical forests.

harass (hăr′ăs; hărăs′) 1. to make a raid upon, with destruction or seizure of property; to lay waste; to raid and ruin; 2. to worry by repeated attacks.

mammoth (măm′ŭth) 1. an elephant no longer living, known by its large teeth and cement-like material be-

90

tween the teeth; 2. referring to size—being very large.

mastodon (măs'tŏ dŏn) an elephant-like animal which is no longer living, differing from a mammoth in the molar teeth.

moraine (mô rān') an accumulation or collection of earth, stones, and debris deposited by a glacier.

navigable (năv'ĭ gá b'l) capable of being used by ships and vessels, deep enough and wide enough to allow boats to pass through.

Nobel Prize (nō bĕl' prīz) a prize or award given to people who work for the interests of humanity in a variety of fields, such as science, medicine, peace, education, literature.

open-pit mine (ō'pĕn-pĭt mīn) a mine in an opening of the earth's surface.

palisades (păl'ĭ sādz') a line of bold cliffs in a high area or in mountains.

pinnacle (pĭn'á k'l) a tall, slender, pointed mass, especially a lofty peak.

portage (pōr'tĭj) the act of carrying boats, goods, etc., overland between navigable waters; also the route over which they are so carried.

raze (rāz) 1. to scrape, cut, or shave off; to erase; 2. to lay level with the ground; demolish; destroy.

relics (rĕl'ĭks) ruins; things left.

sediment (sĕd'ĭ mĕnt) the matter which settles to the bottom from a liquid; material left after water has receded.

temper (tĕm'pẽr) to regulate, especially by moderating; bringing into a more balanced condition.

voyageur (vwä'yä'zhũr') 1. a traveler in Canada and North-Central United States, a man employed by fur companies in transporting goods and men to and from remote areas; 2. any boatman or trapper of those regions.

watershed (wô'tẽr shĕd') 1. the whole region or area making up the supply of a river or lake; 2. a ridge dividing one drainage area from another.

Grateful acknowledgment is made to the following for the helpful information and materials furnished by them used in the preparation of this book:

United States Department of the Interior, National Park Service; particularly Isle Royale National Park and its management.

United States Department of Commerce, Bureau of the Census, Field Services, Chicago, Illinois.

Illinois Departmental Information Service.

Indiana Department of Commerce and Public Relations.

Isle Royale Natural History Association.

State of Michigan Department of Industrial and Economic Development.

Minnesota Division of Publicity, Department of Business Development.

State of Ohio Department of Industrial and Economic Development.

The State of Wisconsin Legislative Reference Library.

International Visual Educational Services, Inc., Chicago, Illinois.

Index

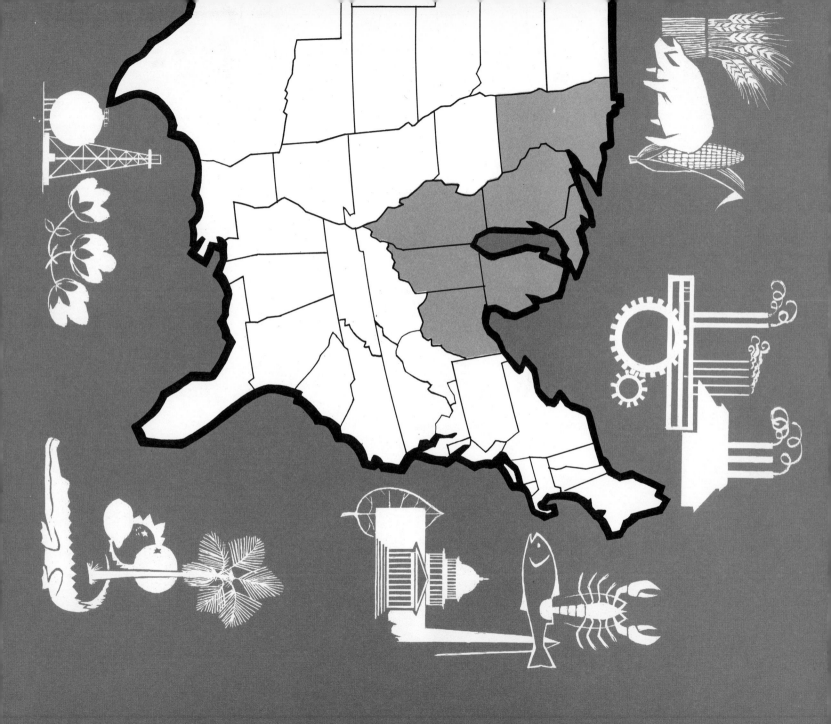